Purpose and Meaning

in

Job

Introduction

Within a shell of some of the greatest poetry ever written lies a sustained meditation on the nature of suffering: why the good suffer and where meaning lies within prolonged pain.

As a structure (and as has often been related), the Book of Job is as extraordinary as its contents. According to its late medieval versification it consists of 42 chapters overall. The first two and the last frame the magnificent poetic sections with what is almost wooden prose. Within the poetic *corpus* the dialogues vary in character. The central character of Job is given to utter some of the highest art whereas his "comforters'" scripts are more workaday, as befits both what they say and the way they say it.

In the original there is the contrast in the sentiments between the Job speeches and those of his companions and I attempt to retain that in some of the clichèd banality of the companions' renderings. Thus the reader will discern that whereas Job's treatment of his own condition is highly sophisticated and nuanced whilst retaining his respect for God, that of his companions is often simplistic, sweeping, deeply unsympathetic and uncaring. The verse given to the young Elihu to speak is not unlike what you might expect from a young articulate person: truthful but not always delivered as an older person would: at times loud, at times lacking in subtlety, showing a certain exasperation at the words of the older persons present and yet with plenty of honesty. Again I have tried to reflect something of this in the current presentation. The pinnacle of the work is contained in the explosive utterances of the Divine, given towards the end.

The original language is indeed Hebrew but Hebrew with a twist: the writer uses both many words not used elsewhere in the bible as well as suffixes and borrowings from other languages amongst them Aramaic, Akkadian and Arabic. Contemporary translations into English themselves make use of other ancient translations into languages other than Hebrew to help make sense of the frequently dense original and I feel some of my renderings will undoubtably show signs of these alternative readings.

Hebrew poetry rarely makes use of discernible rhyme. Instead devices such as simile, parallel verses of meaning either of intensification or contrast, as well as stress and metre, are seen. Furthermore whilst we might always sense what the writer is writing about, the exact illusions can at times be obscure or appear to have more than one meaning. It is not always clear that the extant text has survived intact.

This present rendering is not a translation and should not be considered to be biblical scripture. There are some excellent modern translations available and one in particular, has been created with extraordinary scholarship and fidelity to the text. A short annotated bibliography is given at the end.

It can be challenging to make the translation of an ancient work reflect a more contemporary thought world; the sentiments and ideas of the original, might be difficult to render in the language and culture of another day. This present work is an attempt to freely conceptualise the original, in contemporary language. Thus where for example the original speaks of the anguish at the loss of loved ones, and uses imaginary that would have worked when first written, this work seeks to do something similar in words that might be more intelligible today. In keeping with the original and indeed with some contemporary poetic practice, rhyme is used sparingly.

There is a pulse moving through the lines. I attempt at times to layer the references and allusions. On rare occasions I explicitly borrow from other languages but not on the scale of the original. A reader following both this text and a translation of the original will perceive similar movements from subject to subject and the chapter and verse notations are meant to aid this.

The Passion and work of Christ is alive in this text. For Job, the excruciating painful skin; the terrible thirst; the being forsaken by those you thought were friends; the apparently godly telling you that you are in the wrong and have been forsaken; the sense of having been utterly forsaken by God. All these survived by Job are waiting for their fulfilment in Jesus in that week racing towards Golgotha. Again, in Elihu's contributions: see for example from 33.10 to the end of that chapter.

Some commentators have refused to make these connections and I feel sure many will believe such additions make this into an explicitly Christian work of theology. I hope further consideration will temper such sentiments. A British person hearing Elgar's Nimrod would surely not fail to remember its associations with the yearly Remembrance. Likewise it must be almost impossible not to see similarities between for example Job 16.10 and Isaiah 50.6 (and then with certain of the associated Christian so-called "New Testament" writings).

The book commences with the scene being set for the main verse sections by the so-called 'framing narrative' of chapters 1 and 2. It concludes with a similar but far shorter section in chapter 42, which I have here named the 'Epilogue'. I am quite unsure whether one should follow the majority opinion and consider these to be the additions of a less skilled later editor or compiler: such is the brilliance and unalloyed flamboyance of the writer of the core, that it would seem arrogant to suggest they were not in complete intentionality, entirely capable of what is written, to shell it.

The text concerns, as many will know, the suffering of the righteous, of the good and concerned, caring person. Many of us will know of such people. It seems quite unreasonable for a person 'who does not deserve *this*' to suffer in a profound manner. Job is not the only biblical text to address this subject. Psalm 73 does as well and in the so-called *Akedah* of Genesis 22 many have found similar themes explored. Yet the prime and central example is that of Jesus Christ, who suffered innocent of any and all charges. As the text, the writer to Job and the author of Psalm 73 understand, the resolution to our confusion is only to be found in an ever deeper relationship with the Creator, with God who Himself suffers so unimaginably in the death of God Himself, his son Jesus. In every place where this tragic mystery is addressed, those undergoing these awful events fall progressively silent. This strange and paradoxical truth is explored in a contemporary work by W H Vanstone, 'The Stature of Waiting': the Christ becomes passive in the face of unimaginable suffering. The resolution in each case is a vision of God, a declaration that the person concerned is somehow in God's Presence: Psalm 73 in speaking of the observed injustice says "when I tried to understand this, it was too painful for me, until I entered God's sanctuary". Job in chapter 42, speaks of God appearing to him. These are private encounters. They leave observers feeling frequently unsatisfied whilst confirming their hearers, hearers such as Job, in their trust and faith in God. There we must leave it; such are the facts.

TAPW

202110 with a revised introduction and layout

Table of Contents

1

There was a man in the land of Uz, whose name was Job. That man was blameless and upright, and one who feared God, and turned away from evil. There were born to him seven sons and three daughters. His possessions also were seven thousand sheep, three thousand camels, five hundred yoke of oxen, five hundred female donkeys, and a very great household; so that this man was the greatest of all the children of the east. His sons went and held a feast in the house of each one on his birthday; and they sent and called for their three sisters to eat and to drink with them. It was so, when the days of their feasting had run their course, that Job sent and sanctified them, and rose up early in the morning, and offered burnt offerings according to the number of them all. For Job said, "It may be that my sons have sinned, and renounced God in their hearts." Job did so continually. 10

Now on the day when God's sons came to present themselves before God, Satan also came among them. God said to Satan, "Where have you come from?" Then Satan answered God, and said, "From going back and forth in the earth, and from walking up and down in it." God said to Satan, "Have you considered my servant, Job? For there is no one like him in the earth, a blameless and an upright man, one who fears God, and turns away from evil." Then Satan answered God, and said, "Does Job fear God for nothing? Haven't you made a hedge around him, and around his house, and around all that he has, on every side? You have blessed the work of his hands, and his substance is increased in the land. But stretch out your hand now, and touch all that he has, and he will renounce you to your face." God said to Satan, "Indeed now all that he has is in your power. Only on his person you may not stretch out your hand." So Satan went out from the presence of God. 20

It happened that on a particular day when his sons and his daughters were eating and drinking wine in their oldest brother's house, that a messenger came to Job, and said, "The oxen were plowing, and the donkeys feeding beside them, and the Sabeans attacked, and took them away. They have killed the servants with the edge of the sword, and I alone have escaped to tell you." While he was still speaking, there another also came, and said, "The fire of God has fallen from the sky, and has burned up the sheep and the servants, and consumed them, and I alone have escaped to tell you." While he was still speaking, there also came yet another, and said, "The Chaldeans made three bands, and swept down on the camels, and have taken them away, yes, and killed the servants with the sword; and I alone have escaped to tell you." While he was still speaking, there came another, and said, "Your sons and your daughters were eating and drinking wine in their oldest brother's house, and see here, there came a great storm from the desert, and struck the four corners of the house, and it fell on the young men, and they are dead. I alone have escaped to tell you." 30 40

Then Job arose, and tore his robe, and shaved his head, and fell down on the ground, and worshiped. He said, "Naked I came out of my mother's womb, and naked will I return there. God gave, and God has taken away. Blessed be the name of the Lord." In all this, Job didn't sin, nor charge God with wrongdoing.

2

Again, on the day when the God's sons came to present themselves before God, Satan came also among them to present himself before God. God said to Satan, "Where have you come from?" Satan answered God, and said, "From going back and forth in the earth, and from walking up and down in it." God said to Satan, 50

"Have you considered my servant Job? For there is no one like him in the earth, a blameless and an upright man, one who fears God, and turns away from evil. He still maintains his integrity, although you incited me against him, to ruin him without cause." Satan answered God, and said, "Skin for skin. Yes, all that a man has he will give for his life. But stretch out your hand now, and touch his bone and his flesh, and he will renounce you to your face." God said to Satan, "Indeed now he is in your hand. Only spare his life." So Satan went out from the presence of God, and struck Job with painful sores from the sole of his foot to his head. He took for himself a fragment of a pot to scrape himself with, and he sat among the ashes. Then his wife said to him, "Do you still maintain your integrity? Renounce God, and die." But he said to her, "You speak as one of the foolish women would speak. What? Shall we receive good at the hand of God, and shall we not receive evil?" In all this Job didn't sin in his speaking.

Now when Job's three friends heard of all this evil that had come on him, they each came from his own place: Eliphaz the Temanite, Bildad the Shuhite, and Zophar the Naamathite; and they made an appointment together to come to sympathise with him and to comfort him. When they looked-up and saw him from a distance, and didn't recognise him, they raised their voices, and wept; and they each tore his robe, and sprinkled dust on their heads toward the sky. So they sat down with him on the ground a whole seven days and seven nights, and no one spoke a word to him, for they saw that his grief was very great.

3

This man al-right by his own measure;

in pain;

his lifespan now in flight;

is crashed agin his own being been,

his even being born:

Job opened his mouth, and said:

3.3

"To the memory of that day,

I add my vomit:

the day I was borne out;

the day I was delivered to a world that spits at me now;

blood slimed me then, eased my way;

its draining out:

terminal it had much better been;

no pain, no nothing, at my emptying;

why was there joy at my heralding?

why any tears at my deliverance?

save them for my translating to a painless nothing.

3.6

Trash that entry in time's line!

a date from nought in this globe's endless falling

on its captured path;

let its pointless being, likewise be pointlessly unseen;

a space create,

in the whole calendar carve.

3.11

Tumbling; pointless;

with those tyrants who piled in shifting soil;   100

with the monied who in stupid joy thought to cross the river bagged within their aural palaces;

happy, happy in my confinèd failure

I would have been;

a place where the evil no victims can divest,

and rest is found for those whose rest escaped.

3.13

All at ease together:

the frail, the vain, gold-veined, the pained:

all at rest;   110

the fine, the bound, the frowned, the bold:

all at rest.

3.20

Why light the cave of suffering pain?

why brighten blighted black?

I long to not be here,

and yet 'here' smirks at my futile clinging.

3.22

(My friend I know is released in death;

life confined and death set free).   120

3.24

Things prolonging my living are become fears to me:

my tears answer sustaining drink

and crippling cramp when food appears;

frames I screen in my mind's eye,

become footage my enemies enjoy;

these voyeurs feasting on my darkest sights."

4

Then Eliphaz the Temanite answered:

4.2   130

can you pause a while

to question your own rant?

just long enough to let patience entertain?

you've trashed your words,

how could I not come back?

4.3

you've referred many,

kept the small afloat and the underfunded going;

plodding they are and plodding you were,

yet they keep going and all this has now struck you;   140

and so your smug inner has been peeled-back;

what you despaired of in them

has appeared between your sheets!

4.5

come-on: you spoke to them of faith,

and yet now faith has turned on you!

should not faith - in your words - dissolve fate in you?

4.7

you know the rule:

do good to make god work for you;   150

where have you heard of the good rubbed-out?

that little person slated?

you know I know and all know:

if you do good,

then good enfolds you;

so stand not against the good,

to save that sticky end;

rights' might is justice I'm sure;

might alone has blown their right to Right's justice;

the powerful and their kin: 160

all alike kindle nature's gaia;

4.12

A whispered hint was all it was,

a mere dint in the silence;

yet it grew out of all reason as does panic in the night;

in dark dreams even nonsense casts a shadow;

yet this materièl stepped out of the unreal

and in reality caused my flame to shake;

a spectre felt, not seen, which creeped my skin;

4.16   170

I stopped and waited for its form

but only sound shaped its words:

"full right you might want to appear

but can a woman be justified before divinity;

a man be pure in the sight of its Maker?".

4.19

If unreal materièl he does not trust,

how much less the human being who turns to dust?

Less value than a moth,

so little that scores   180

are lost unseen between our meals,

and that full waxed in age and height

yet full waned in mind and wisdom;

these not even forgotten,

for they were never even known.

5

5.1

So ring the bell, but who will answer?

Which divine will lance your boils,

your lonely cries attend?   190

5.2

Anger and envy consume both fool and idiot;

I saw their houses, their roots, their branches,

and despised their feebleness, their frailties:

their children fared no better:

fraudster and nature take their share:

this is the idiots' allotment:

not born but earned.

5.8

But I know better!   200

I follow God and appeal to Him;

Divinity is unsearchable, unfathomable;

wonders never cease from His hand;

raining blessings everywhere:

on the humble, the bowed down,

the sorrowful and plated-full alike.

5.13

That fraudster is defrauded, success eludes,

the clever caught in their own knots;

like experts they are become fools,   210

sunlight leading them only into blindness

and Divinity divines their play

to deliver the played from their hand.

Hope prises open the palm of the hopeless,

levering open the plug in the arrogant's vessel;

happiness parallels His reproof

since Divine discipline delights!

Soreness and salve: both He hands out,

harshness and healing the two He pairs.

From distress, from famine and from war: 220

from each and every one you are relieved;

I laugh at violence and assault,

whether from animal or my kind.

So to my travels, a time away,

yet to my home in peace I shall return I know alway:

my home, my base, my 'family':

all these will I know, increase.

Even at my death I will be strong still:

my ideas, my progeny, remain;

this is how truth is: 230

life works this way,

I do declaim.

6

Job replies to Eliphaz:

                                                                    6.2

The needle of the balance

would nere approach the vertical,

were this anguish and all my pain,

set against the earth's mass weighed against it.

                                                        6.3   240

My words are unmeasured,

so too the Almighty's arrows finding me;

my venom matching their venom,

both sapping, grinding down my vigour;

the vinegar and gall of His terror

glowering over my embers;

                                                                    6.6

The taste,

the very odour of food,

floods me with bile;   250

oh that he would allow,

this my waste to flow out as I fade away:

"Let go my thread and let me go!".

6.10

But his life, his word, I will not release,

nor permit my bile against his command to cease.

I'm no iron pillar or bronze wall;

what am I and how small my strength

that I should this endure!

with my hope hiding and fighting faith fading.   260

6.14

Why won't you help; why won't you comfort?

why won't you cry my tears with me?

Hold-up my end,

that my end with God might be secure!

let me not fade away in despair.

6.15

Instead of your tears,

I've tasted the drought of your comfort:

stinking congealed puddles,   270

under an unrelenting scorching heat.

As I pump for your sympathy,

your wells have run dry;

Your words turn-in on themselves:

blind alleys for those seeing

beyond their little hedges;

mere mirages to the many who longed-for,

cried-out for, screamed,

implored for, something,

some crumb.   280

6.23

I've not asked these friends

for wealth or armies to defend me;

no deliverance from a fraudster or tormentor:

just a crumb, a something, for my comfort.

6.24

Now, silence me with your truth,

my thrashing meanderings with correcting wisdom!

I would bear the bitterness of loving reproof,

yet yours is but backspacing bitching;   290

where is your authority?

your grace? your gift of justice?

The bereaved, the bereft, these you sell-out;

it's all for gain and gold with you.

6.28

Look me in the eye,

to your faces I will not lie;

come about, come to me: truth is here!

My way is right,

my scales secure   300

against the blight of inequity;

7

7.1

The grinding drag, the unreleavèd strain, the pain;

these the members of the working gang

expect their contracts to enforce;

days starting in shadow,

longing for the 'tock' of off;

so to earn, so to re-turn;

to pay, to turn about, to earn.   310

7.3

And you who make?

neither pause, nor turn away;

my nightly pain I drown

and stay my course and my cause not own.

7.4

Is not my bed a refuge?

so why the damp, the cold,

the mess of spreads and covers;

the terrors of un-sleep?   320

                                                    7.5

My skin without betrays my times within:

cracked and worn,

with vile little fiery friends visiting,

like you,

sapping what thin sap remains.

                                                    7.6

And so my time speeds ticking past so fast,

that days end with lagging hope,

held back as if life forsakes so light a breath,   330

and happiness fails to alight

on something so swiftly moving.

                                                    7.8

I'm sought,

but even sight lags the place of my speeding;

homes and chattels, hopes and longings,

                                                    7.9

just clouds,

and in passing are passed into forever un-knowing;

The rank sickness of this lost right,   340

to home, to friends, to memory,

                                                    7.11

makes my voice, this screaming,

this pained hollering,

sound in that raging pit:

marred, pickled, smarting, acid:

it barks.

                                                    7.12

Why cage me in:

my mind, my flesh?   350

Why bar the way to my easing?

Why open my mind's sluice,

to dreams and terrors?

Throttled death,

is sweeter than eked-out un-living!

My life is lathed away,

shaving but tiny amounts al-way:

I hate it: move away! 360

Leave-off the holding of my thread,

it is but smoke.

What are we?

Why seek us out?

Why chase us, challenge us,

morning, noon and night?

Leave! leave-off just long enough,

for a snatched breath,

a mouthful of scratched sustaining; 370

Have I enlivened evil - is it that?

Targeted the killing of good,

as justice for your holding me in sight?

Has my lying and fraud wearied you,

become a weight to heavy for you to bear?

So then: be gracious and forgive!

Be merciful and erase;

I'm fading fast:

You'll hunt for me, 380

but I'll be long ceased.

8

Bildad, raising his voice, spoke-up:

8.2

You speak, but for how long?

You move the air, but to what purpose?

8.3

Does God upset the ways of justice,

confound the righteous path?

8.4   390

Your children did wrong and suffered the penalty;

yet now, even now,

turn and open your life to His mercy;

plead with Him;

pursue purity and his path,

and the machinations of the most high

will engage the automata of justice;

your future flourishing

will shade the memory of their passing.

8.8   400

Ask your generations

and delve into your family's wisdom:

what do we ourselves know,

mere shadows against the line of time,

whispers firstly heard but yesterday?

Yet they will speak to you,

pouring their collected words into your inner ear.

Nature draws its life from the Lord,

revealing its ways as mirrors of His hand;

what, who, can live, severed from its base?

410

8.13

And such an end comes on any who forget their God,

blaspheming against the way of things,

8.15

trusting in what they themselves have built,

partying on shaking rafters;

young and thrusting,

vivacious and bright;

the trap, it trips!

And another victim rises by return. 420

8.18

You are not missed,

you were never even known.

8.20

The Lord neither rejects the pure,

nor seeks out the putrid;

8.21

hilarity and happiness:

both are in His gift;

8.22   430

hate Him and less than a hint of you remains.

9

Job answers Bildad:

9.2

Yes true, its true,

yet how to be true to Truth?

And who can challenge Truth and Knowledge,

still less survive the bout?

Would my clashing words parry One whose breath

flails these plates? 440

9.6

One who sets both orb and orbits?

where light and dark matter so little,

that we are played in unknowing knowledge?

9.8

All energy are the oceans,

fumed upon the shore,

answering the heavens' call,

so making our clocks

worth their ticking, 450

in great spreadings of the heavens,

He is creating;

9.10

Divinity is unsearchable, unfathomable:

wonders never cease from His hands;

9.11

passing,

He passes by unseen,

my perceiving being upon a different plane;

what He parses of life and living,   460

none can resist or answer;

His purpose no purpose of ours can turn or refract,

nor pull back His hand 'till it pauses;

9.14

And so this is true and I cannot answer Truth,

nor stand against such knowledge;

though charge-less,

if charged by Him to reply,

I would, facing His majesty,

His terror, be charged down.   470

9.16

If I call,

why should He pick-up?

or in faining to reply,

why should he choose choicest over blemished?

the crushed fruits of my life being all I'm left,

as after hail upon the vine.

9.18

Leave-off just long enough

for that one snatched breath!   480

I've drunk your bitter acid and it has sieved me;

of strength there is no battle,

in neither ring nor court.

9.20

Though charge-less,

if charged to reply,

my twisted, holed innards,

are dying upon their feet,

leaving my medium of air,

no harvest to reply.   490

9.21

I am blameless,

yet decimated without a charge!

my crying quaking me,

making me loose my mind:

What are we? Who am I?

9.22

One and all are alike,

the One He crushes:

the Perfect One and the liar;   500

9.23

when God acts by Act of God,

one and all are alike,

their flow of life ebbs away:

the Perfect One and the liar;

As with life,

so with living:

9.24

justice escapes the timid,

the bribe of the wealthy   510

hooding the eyes of those who judge;

yet the Judge of all the earth,

goes about hooded and cloaked,

surely ignoring us all;

bears He no guilt (by omission)?

9.25

And so my days slip by,

running,

running at such speed that even joy cannot join,

and the ribbon's gone   520

before the conductor's call.

Yet before the whirling of my draining life,

sucks away my bitter complaining,

the memorised pain holds it all awaiting,

like a rotting morsel,

played upon the grating.

And why should I

let my guilt thin me out?

Save for You, its surely proven

in the furnace of my gout'd cov'ring;   530

(my self-improvement guru urged a change of plan:

a bit of joy, involve a smile perhaps?

but all that collapsed in my screaming reality) -

                                                    9.30

If I should weigh and let drift to a fresher place,

Your anchor holds me fast,

and adds fresh ordure as reward for my campaigning.

You are not one of me,

you need not answer any summons I might make,

since who could sit bewigged above us?   540

                                                    9.34

There is no clerk or gaoler

who could lay a hand

upon your shoulder.

No one can compel You to answer for:

your little friends,

your gall,

your wracking,

this stinking cracking skin;

these companions,   550 your terrors;

and fear would run,

and I would speak.

9.35

But I ramble and this is not to be.

10

I am thinned out,

my thread is frayed;

all that's left is acid and anger and it has said:

10.2   560

Condemn me not!

still, I am sentenced by your lashings of ripping pain;

Why do you do it?

What is the point?

I was made by you!

Why strip your own skin?!

what's the pleasure - seeing the stripped original,

while Injustice around the back,

asset strips the Works, the homes,

the shirts of those whom Justice should uphold!

570

10.4

All seeing See'er,

why do you permit it?

Has the lighting failed in heaven?

Your seeing and your years are not like ours,

that you should take delight,

as our evil does.

10.7

I am innocent!

but there is no clerk or gaoler

who might lay a hand upon your shoulder.

10.8

I am made in your mould,

assembled in your works,

why take me apart

with no credit

to your charge?

Fashioning, you fashioned me,

building both frame and the framing of it;

what pleasure is there in crushing,   590

to crush it?

                                                    10.15

Such is my ravaged psuche,

that were I guilty,

my fate sways in front of me,

yet if guiltless,

this crushing prevents me

from rising in my spirit,

and emptied, I fall back again.

                                        10.16   600

Still;

why bother?

for should you see my horizaned spirit,

shots fired would faultlessly hit their mark,

in total, accurate, supremacy.

                                        10.17

Accusers: their witness multiplying;

rank upon rank folding over the horizon.

                                        10.18

Why oh why was my passage eased from the womb?   610

It would have pained me nothing then,

to be emptied-out in that room.

                                        10.20

And now though my days are rushing by,

and thin in number.

"Loose me! leave me!

that I may locate some crumb of rest!"

10.21

And then to leave,

an eternal wanderer,

in no-time shadow,

death forever,

disrupted, dismal, disorder.

620

11

11.2

Then Zohar the Naamathite spoke up and said:

So many many words from you!

lippy for sure,

yet with but lip-service to Truth.

Who gives credence to such babbling?

Is this true Creedal might

when you make light

of others' right talking?

630

11.4

You make a pitch for the all-Right,

in speech, in deed:

pleading in purity to the One,

with paired flailing to quiet of the other;

11.5

yet would but the One,

reverse your lips,

and return true wisdom;

the One facing earth and heaven:

in gracious mercy and sacred purity;

640

11.7

Who has permit,

to divine that vine of complete divinity;

Your highest and perfection

'gainst our mediocre waiverings?

All universal sight and scope divine,

'gainst our seeing crabbed close,

in dimmed veniality.

11.10

No court can confine

or preventive order ensnare

the One Divine;

yet snare will He deceit,

and sign that order to confine

that evil defining bad as fine.

11.12   660

Be as Issachar;

be earth's salt, God's gift,

and claim gifted wisdom,

for your loyalty.

11.13

So offer Him your fealty,

hands in stretched obeisance;

throw away your treachery,

leach lecherous veniality,

11.15   670

and only one vision will fill your frame;

no fear, no scourge, no blemish,

will blight your name,

and troubles from you will flee;

11.17

as waters spinning down,

so light beyond bright will flood your life;

your murky morn

switching to blistering noon.

11.18   680

Your peace in hope is cemented-in,

your rest in safety, made secure.

Fear will flee,

and many will decree:

"your word is truth!";

Evil's slaves will not escape

Hell's gaping hole,

and with fading hope,

that final grasp on life,   690

ends in gasping wracking breath.

12

Then Job responded:

12.2

Yes, I will admit!

You really are the piece:

'Bastions of truth!',

wisdom sees you and dies!

12.3

But I am no slouch,   700

and bright with you;

I know these things,

your equals too.

12.4

Am I a joke,

'cos I walked to Him,

and He me crushed

on my returning?

And so are all

who without fault and blameless be.   710

Reposing, vile flaming

the pure in their calamity,

and assisting innocence to trip.

12.6

Their mansions rise,

their gold piled high,

helped by Him

who ought to trip them

in their carnality.

12.7   720

Yet - argh! - I know

in pain a truth:

go ask the animals,

they can teach us;

the birds, the very earth they cover,

so too the contents of the sea:

it knows,

that God has done all this,

the life and breath of all are His.

12.11   730

Each to its task:

the tongue for taste,

the ear to hear,

so too wisdom with the aged,

with them is understanding;

12.13

power and wisdom rest in God,

discernment and right judgement,

are with Him;

12.14   740

where God acts, such is finality:

in destruction, destroyed,

in detention, without end;

water: in lack or plenty,

both weapons to spend;

12.16

the Lord sustains feast and famine,

king and carpenter,

sagacity and stupidity.

12.17   750

The arrogant in their judgements,

the wise in their wisdom:

for one its trousers down,

and for the other,

wreckage in the calamity of events.

12.18

Divinity both binds and frees,

those both free and bound;

prelate to pauper,

and ranked to ranker,   760

none should before God

presume to retain

either speech or wisdom,

power or precedence;

12.22

Death is uncovered

cowering in its lair;

those in grave's shadow,

brought out rejoicing.

12.23   770

Nations are caught in the bellows:

puffed-up in greatness,

sucked empty as they expire,

their wide borders now meeting,

emptying their hope.

12.24

Leaders, orphaned of sense,

panic and flee,

and in the desert of failure,

no exit they see;   780

thrashing in darkness,

their absence unknown.

13

13.1

All this, all this,
I know, I've seen;

13.2

I am no slouch and bright like you,
I know these things, your equals too.

13.3   790

Divinity: vast, bright, beyond, almighty:
to God I call;
"Liars all through", I call you,
"Quilters of wind", I dub you:
fall silent! that's wisdom indeed!

13.6

Do you not presume?
Do you not assume?
This is now my brief,
so hear now my case: 800

13.7

Do you divine the thinking of Divinity
wrecking righteousness: speaking infamy?
Do you side with Him,
who no side decrees
and in your flattery,
lick, spin, kowtow,
always nattily alighting
on that division,
which you suppose   810
will make Him
well disposed t'ward you,
who could not survive
the wracking He might impose
on you: lick-spitting lacky,

who does rather depose

a fact, a line, a truth,

than clinging shaking to verity?

13.11

That of His majesty and His terror   820

makes wits to fly

yet passes by you

who have no wit

to stand to reply.

13.13

So save your wind,

let me be

that I may speak:

let it come!

yet why do I expose my flank   830

my me?

To such danger,

my life imperilled be;

13.15

yet such is my faith in Him

that death may come

yet Him my champion

I shall see

and Hope will proclaim

in thundering clarion peels   840

my victory.

13.16

I will to defend my case

and so to Him I face

and in this act

will see me saved

for no two-faced

can God see,

and live.

13.17   850

And now alive to Him

this whole being

unwraps, unfolds,

to You this mystery

this riddle

in my place:

13.18

my brief (not short)

is that I am right

and in the right   860

place, for who would contend with me?

And in my contempted place,

let me expirèd be.

13.20

This crushing and this fear

me awakes to know Your presence near,

such meaning:

I should not my face submit to hiding,

13.21

if you would but   870

abate your hiding of me

in terror and afright;

so in removing,

restrain that palm,

that biting cane,

and with it the terror

that attends its whipping.

13.22

Now call and I will answer

or I enquire and you reply: 880

what are my sins and their number?

Point to my errors, that hunger to offend!

Why hide your face

and declare offence between us,

when I am but a breath

and tinder to your thunder?

13.26

For the acid of your writ

recalls the truth of youthful faults

and for these am I now in irons   890

and watched in fine detail,

to the tracking of all my days,

and the branding of my hide?

13.28

And so I rot

and waste away,

a feast for moth and worm.

14

14.1

Though our days are but brief,   900

our troubles are not ever;

as a flower, so we pass,

as a shadow, barely there.

14.3

is it worthy of Your gaze to transfix such a one?

to haul me out and drag me down?

14.4

to attempt to clean that which is sourced from Not?

14.5

You both do the numbers and them make;   910

so days are created,

and me made for each,

and them counted,

so on the next I do not wake.

14.6

Look away, look away and restrain your beating,

'till days be counted,

my contract's ceasing - and my days so ending.

14.7

But how different are we   920

if considered 'gainst other created things!

A tree cut down will come again,

its death, not death but feigning;

in old age it re-creates,

shooting out new life,

death abating.

14.10

What of us?

we live, we age,

power flees, we expire,   930

we are not less, not old,

just not;

14.12

tides come, waters flow,

empires rise, nations go,

moons wax and stars implode,

but us?

Just not.

14.13

Secrete me in your hidden halls,   940

hide me 'till your terror trawls my counted days,

then at the next bring me to your gaze,

and lift me from the dead.

14.14

Do we not surely rise?

Thus this me sustains through my bloodied paining,

until thrice dawned I'm pulled alive from my ruin;

14.15

then to your calling, I will answer,

stripped pure, I will be sought, 950

Your creation replying to its father;

to my numbers from before you add my steps now rightly shod,

and my former sins from your memory are now taken,

secreted, sealed,

forbidden to be re-entered in your book.

14.18

The mountain roars:

its pelts of snow, ice and earth

are ripped away;

the river roars: 960

its torrents rip, trip and gouge

its bed and edgings,

dragging them to parts afar.

So too for us:

death sweeps all away,

your power displayed and we and hope depart,

a ravaged corpse remaining sole witness to posterity's

honours and defaming;

14.22

so he mourns his pain 970

and mourns alone.

15

Then Eliphaz the temanite answered:

15.2

Were you wise,

your talk would not waft and thin,

(your words: whimpering wisps,

weightless though weighty in tone)

you would value your talk,

over witless twitter; 980

15.4

yet so poor, so light,

so you damage

and may way-lay those

whose delight is to wait upon the Lord!

15.5

Your words spiral and twist,

down and round,

feeding themselves,

teaching sound minds,   990

to dissent and to rebel.

15.6

In proof I call your mouth as witness,

bagging wind and crowning arrogance:

15.7

are you the world's first to be born,

conducting the hills in their rising?

15.8

Did you earwig the Almighty's hushed councils,

trapping all His gushings of wisdom?   1000

15.9

We do not slouch,

we're bright beyond you,

we know things,

more equal than you.

15.10, 11

Trace the aged,

and they will affirm,

with us they side and do confirm,

your father's father they knew,   1010

and now are quick to say,

that you slay God's tender mercies and ridicule

His graceful gentleness and consoling care.

15.12

Yet violence of speaking,

your visage shouting,

betrays your rage at the Divine,

who is surely only seeking

a motivating purity from any and all of His creating;

15.15   1020

and if unreal materièl He does not trust,

how much less

the human being

who returns to dust?

15.16

who unforgiven and unforgiving

sprinkles unjust acts,

on all their days,

like confetti at a wedding.

15.17   1030

So let me explain

take it from this one who can declare,

what the wise declaim in openness and full clarity;

15.19

to whom God alone gifted where you stand,

this land no vreemd one

did pollute with looted gods

from Canaan's past.

15.20

The one who casts aside all purity: 1040

tormented be their days,

their ways, with no delivr'ance,

for this fraudster,

this tormentor!

No crumb, no comfort do they possess,

15.21

save times of violence on languid summer days,

which for others do caress,

their families in peace and play,

as at a beach, a pool.   1050

15.22

Yet for the hacker, the thief, the robber?

hack-off of their ways from this earth!

and slimy doorways:

dank, dark and rank,

nibbled toes and only fitful, terrorised, repose;

a brief pause,

then forever darkness enfolds.

15.25

The one who would suppose to oppose the Divinity,   1060

who thought themselves before,

high, above, beyond all other mortality

and saw fit in word and deed

to launch attacks upon mere humanity;

wallowing in aural splendour,

15.27

fat on others' prosperity:

iceberg'd palaces they built!

All glittering and sparkling hues,

for show above, for one,   1070

resting upon,

crushing down the ninety-nine who built the thing,

whose wealth he stole,

which wealth cannot cling,

for from his final cave

he will slink to death,

facing opaque, cold, soulless eternity,

howling furnaces, chasing eternally.

15.30

And so the Creator's breath   1080

takes back His gift of days.

15.31

So do not trust what does not endure:

it lies, it cheats, it fogs your inclinations:

godless not God becoming your destination.

15.34

Yet long before your Watcher removes

what you did misuse,

(your garden, your plantings, your posterity),

these falter;   1090

not apples but acid drops

will fall and all your deliveries,

your product,

will only call to mind your stupidity

in wanting 'things' not company;

licking flames will in their rage,

consume all your ways:

your bribery, your fraud, your corrupted thinking.

15.35

From cradle to grave: 1100

stinking, oozing, yellow:

it stuck fast, and never, ever, left you.

16

Then Job replied:

16.2

Here is no mystery,

no profundity,

neither originality nor cutting simplicity.

All has been heard before.

What misery you deliver,   1110

cloaking these draughty words;

"soothing, comforting utterances",

but floating windy pillars.

16.3

An ugly beauty in oratory,

negating its intent:

where is the heartfelt base,

that sustains such billowing prose?

16.4

If in your place, 1120

would I let loose such pots of lice

over your embroidered counterpane?

16.5

Might I not place instead

a brace of rods of steel,

of words,

and so enable your embrace

of this adversity?

16.6

But all this is word, 1130

is wind, is breath,

and the pain, its heft,

is here now still;

so I stop, I cease;

but yet no! no release.

16.7

The wearing out,

this thinning fine,

has ripped my home, my kind,

from any plate or base to which in past 1140

it was afixed.

16.8

And so the rake,

this spectre that once me was,

stands to witness this nixing

of that former rude good blessing

that I then fronted

to a world that now laughs at me.

16.9

Your rage,   1150

your anger,

tears and rips;

it gnaws upon my bones,

never wavering in its gaze;

its hooks are never loosed from the lips that hold our eyes in lockèd phase;

16.10

And now the noise, it rises,

the growling, the crowd,

they hit, they beat my one cheek and then the other,

in concert and conspiracy;   1160

they unite in their evil confederacy,

to conspire and accept from God,

this abandoned limpened embodiment of pitiful humanity.

16.12

Shaken in peaceful naivety my frame lies shattered,

neck and stature now a mere target,

a point of aim,

for your surrounding companies.

16.13

Holed, my fluid leaves my smell   1170

upon the ground

16.14

and all my towers, my walls,

bowing repeatedly,

until they crash and fail to your rushing,

your crushing of any remaining failing frame of me.

Any fame or note is gone.

I've skinned carpet and cardboard as my coating;

each failed your assaulting, and now this "me",

my self-noting,   1180

all is buried beneath any notion that I might possess some value,

something others might note,

of worth, of pride,

and puckered, rubbery, tearèd skin and nose,

puffy eyes, deep hollow shadows,

only these remaining.

16.17

Still: no weapons can they find,

no violence at my hands

and my prayers continue to rise unabated   1190

to your highest heavens.

16.18

I am only dust:

but ashes mixed with some blood and bile and other,

so do not, I ask,

cover over such meagre fare,

nor my screaming anechoic make.

You Lord, taste and see, smell and hear;

so now witness this thin rake, from your heaven, be my champion,

my advocate, do not me abandon,   1200

and use my tears, as dammèd waters,

to block, to plead for me;

16.21

as friend, as barrister,

contend 'gainst these mere men,

who stand 'gainst me!

16.22

There is so little time remaining:

for me,

I will descend as all others have before,   1210

from there I am assured,

there is no returning.

17

In stretching, I am broken,

in thinning, I am gone,

the grave's gape awaits me,

their cackling all around me,

no strength to avert my gaze.

17.3

But yet even now,   1220

at this late hour,

put-up the money!

make that deal,

for me, to me,

take my side,

for whom else have I to pay my bond?

since I can see you've opaqued their minds,

and will fail their lives' exam;

17.5

(these the ones   1230

who strip the others

to accrete themselves,

their injustice ripping posterity

from their very own).

17.6

I am the exemplar,

the design, the plan,

they frighten with;

their spit I taste for

they fear to face,   1240

this grief, this injustice

and in me there's

no frame to frame,

and only shadows are remaining.

I am a frightener for the ones

who in their just ways

have pulp for their thinking,

17.8

('cos surely only badness

gives rise   1250

to this creeping,

sapping grieving!?)

17.9

Still, in my mind's eye,

it grows not dim:

this justice seeking

for my right way

and my right thinking;

17.10

So you might turn   1260

and me do face,

but there's no

wisdom, no thought,

nor even space,

that you might vary

your right crooked path,

where my plans lie,

scattered, shattered;

(it's my heart that's flaked,

amongst these shards);   1270

17.12

Your calling of night 'day'

and darkness 'bright',

leaves my hope aiming

solely for a grave,

which will save me

calling your fraud a friend,

your crackling cackle 'a lamp';

Will hope survive?

will it cruise through this gate,   1280

to rise beyond?

Or with me only to the dust relate?

18

18.1

Then Bildad the Shuhite answered:

18.2

Can time wait to hear you pause this rant,

this unending spate of words?

Halt! and now wait for our riposte:

18.3   1290

Who's the fool to think us but asses,

beastial, to your 'higher sight'?

18.4

This anger: it fractions you,

giving vent to such fantasies as 'new orders'

and variant realities:

but rock and stone they do not change,

and this place? it will remain for all our ages.

18.5

This we do know,   1300

it is surely true,

that evil's destiny is written:

its vitality is dulling

and likewise its tacky glint is fading;

its disciples groping in dim burrows,

tripping deftly over their own counsels:

"see, my net of lies will catch,

any number of these minnows",

but lacking connaissance of practicalities,

its weighted cords   1310

drag calamity to lift its gaze

from the shoaling innocent majority,

to pounce upon the fraud,

the liar, the slick talker,

and spinning upon their heel,

their silken pitch now stuttered,

they're pitched headlong

into their privy gutter,

where all their secret terrors

in patience, their victory now claiming -   1320

are expressed upon their opened side:

fires without consume and immune battles rage within,

such being betrayed

as boils, as piles, fissures,

eating pathogens,

and haunted eyes,

with many hours spent in little rooms.

18.17

So the evil fade from memory,

driven nameless from our lives our times;   1330

even of their family,

all gone;

what of their progeny?

We went to search,

to see them in their localities:

all gone.

18.20

All society now gets to know,

that this is how it is with those,

who refuse to own,   1340

their God.

19

19.1

Then Job answered and said:

19.2

Tormenting torrents,

crushing green,

phlegm and spume:

these your words,

their weighing greater   1350

than my lighter frame can hold -

up I must rise to confine my cause,

as mine alone,

though your assaults might seek to draw me in,

                                                    19.5

no higher ground can you claim

by showering me in shame:

a disgrace of your own making!

                                                    19.6

For this net,   1360

this moated life of mine,

is His alone.

                                                    19.7

So I scream for help

but the sole reply

is the echo of mine own crying,

pleading for justice though none arrives.

                                                    19.8

The Lord has hemmed me in on every side:

terrored dark behind,   1370

unscaled mounts surround.

                                                    19.9

Name and honour have vacated

this the place my person once did over-flow.

                                                    19.10

I am the clothe-less at a crowded ball

with no vestry for hope to tailor my return.

                                                    19.11

And so His anger burns afresh.

He must see in me an enemy,   1380

19.12

for His companies in full array,

advance assaulting all I might claim for home,

19.14

for family.

All my relatives have run from me:

no siblings,

no kin remain for my upholding.

They fail - these familiar faces

have obliterated me from their memories! 1390

19.15

Even those in my employ,

I call but have to crawl afore they do my bidding;

and as for these my guests:

they may stare in my direction,

yet me they cannot see.

I am an alien become.

19.17

A dragon's breath they must be smelling,

for they are all repelled: 1400

my wife, no relative,

no child will close with me;

19.18

abuse and insults are hurled from afar,

no lover loves me now;

no friend will sit with me

and in detesting me

sees only this skeleton

clad scantily in skin and flesh;

the thinnest of breaths separating me from death; 1410

19.21

Pity! Pity!

I plead: have pity on me!

Why help God's hand with your own striking?

Surely this my purgatory

is sufficient to satisfy

even your lust for misery?

19.23

Find me a marker which no effort can erase,

write this down and this record, 1420

so that forever no denyer

might an audience entertain

with the fraud

that these wracking pains

were but a play

for an evening paid!

19.25

Now I affirm that God alone

my Redeemer is,

who lives and in my entry into His halls 1430

before His face alone will I stand

and no other occupant there inhabits.

19.27b

And now I'm fading fast and should you ask

where to slice a little more from me,

beware! for those who wield the knife

must know that by that knife

they will be sought

and it will bring calamity.

20

1440

20.1

Then Zophar the Naamathite answered:

(there's no need to change our wisdom,

which from ancient times is forged)

20.2

your revisionings unsettle our base,

that calm foundation,

and my thinking,

quivers at your challenge,

20.3   1450

this presumptuous inversion for

20.4

you know that from of old,

the life of evil,

save briefly blights our communal living;

the successful smell, the flashy bearing,

some clanging gongs, are all but temp'ry,

20.7

(with that whiff too now suspect,

being stuck to its shodding).   1460

And when we went to see their living,

their See, they were not there,

20.8

(the suspicion being that a spectre

had ghosted them away),

20.9

with friends no longer

sensing familiarity in their faces,

20.10

their inheritors taxed for compensation,   1470

20.11

and the dust of their leaving

mixing with that of their cremating.

20.12

So the choices evil makes are there to snare themselves,

the poison they excrete is the venom in their veins;

such opulence that legend writes,

is earned yet nere consumed,

it gorges on the wealth of little ones,

it runs them down and hounds them,   1480

'till their very homes,

their little castle mounds,

are forfeit by the basket-full;

and yet this craving to oppress is never satisfied:

kettleing their prey does not arrest

20.21

this terminal desire

20.22

to eat the country clean

and so a desert bring   1490

to both his psyche and this land;

20.23

Divinity flailing as just deserts

his puddin' from his mains,

20.24

and should the wicked dodge the first,

the second will connect.

20.25

Violent death is waiting there,

and in its succeeding,   1500

flooding home and hearth,

and draining monied wealth.

20.27

See here! Heaven is detailing

all of evils' failings

whilst egging-on the Burgers.

And a great bell for evil tolls,

from eternity condemning.

21

Then Job answered: 1510

21.2

And now do not paint-over your own warpèd thinking;

if you will to stand with me,

hear this now and be to me some true consoling;

21.3

and once my words have passed,

then do deliver your cackling riposte.

Are these my words aimed at one like you?

It is to Him alone I make my plea;

and so cannot expect interpretation,

1520

that makes sense of this my 'august' reputation,

as one whose unique record of utter deprivation,

leaves you aghast and bereft of any observation;

My memories alone quake my frame at this:

the total horror of my plight.

21.7

See here now these evil folk:

they are not slowed upon their upward path!

Their families with them increase,

they thrive,

1530

their generations embedded in their flashy high-rising.

Don't shame yourselves!

These are not caught in any trap:

21.9

no rod, no chastisement from God

awaits their daily frauds.

21.10

"Businesses", they call them!

Wealth cascades from every venture;

holidays with their generations

1540

rewarding their twists and turns within the law.

21.13

And their ends of days? in pain, in terror,

with twisted bowels and tubes and blood and fears?

No! not like us peasants do they die!

In peace they float away to sleep!

21.14

And so of-course they say:
"God? You we do not see!
where is His mark, His place, His walk?   1550
to Him we will not flee!

21.15

who is this "Divine" we are called to see, to serve?
where is the gain
in chasing us to know
the Great Unframed?"

21.16

Like as salt is ground into my scabs,
these sliced hands, these wounds,
so I know that all this their prosperity,   1560
is no accident, not come by their own hand,
(but still I will not wind along their paths, their frauds,
or adopt their filthy lies).

21.17

And do you hear of such ones' accidents?
their deaths before their times?
Does God bind them like me
with no parting from my pains?

21.18

Do you delude yourselves with thoughts of regal laws   1570
which apportion guilt and blame equally
twixed wealth and fame
and notoriety?

21.19

Or perchance it is your thought
that these their parents' fault,
visits their posterity,
whilst in mockery leaving them
to complete their infamy?

21.21   1580

For why should such a one,

give thought, that when they're gone,

some other might own their case

and take their fall?

21.22

But know this:
God's knowledge belongs to God entire;

the Lord needs not us as teachers,

for there is not one

who is not judged by Divinity alone.   1590

21.23

So like with our Lord's Judging,

this Death comes upon us all:

the fit, the fat, the thin, some young, all old,

the crabbed, the bright:

and dust is where we all locate.

21.27

Do you take me for a fool,

not to know of your devising, your scheming,

for your planning is laid bare   1600

when you request reporting of:

"this evil man's housing",

and the place of mes affaires.

21.29

Why think you to understand

the manner of this trading,

this or that firm's accounting,

the deportment of its officers,

the mounting evidence of fraud,

when left to their own devices?   1610

21.30

The evil are not punished!

They long to crush,

to pull the wool, to fleece,

and whose law or officer is paid to bar their way,

to tax them for their crimes?

Nay! not taxed but celebrated are these prime bulls!

and when they die,   1620

countless clammer for a stall,

to eulogise their disgusting idols' dancing,

o'er the mangled poor.

22

Then Eliphaz the Temanite answered:

22.2

Our God grows not rich

trading strength from the strong

or charity from some nunnery;

there's no wealth to be made - had you found some -,   1630

from your purity, correctness, sobriety;

your case is the proof:

your calamity proves your iniquity!

22.4

is Justice a smiter,

Virtue a tankard for woes?

22.5

Thus your terrible end, echoes your friend,

this Evil you must be concealing.

22.6   1640

From the poor you pawned their essentials,

and clothing from those who had none;

22.7

with the food that they had,

you feasted your beasts;

their milk, to your little ones too.

22.8

From your wealth you gave none

to those in the slums

(though these were lodged on your land);   1650

and for sport you pitted the pitiful,

against some of these benighted few.

                                            22.10

So, none is lacking any explanation,

for your torments,

your pains and your wracking;

                                            22.11

and for why these floods of terrors,

are you now overwhelming.

                                            22.12   1660

God occupies the highest heaven,

beyond the furthest stars,

                                            22.13

and yet you still pose the question:

"what can He see, perceive, from afar?

The Divine we know, is so way beyond all our vision,

our treads do not meet, and this separation meaning,

'God above and us below - we're divided in all our living'".

                                            22.15

And so you fail to recall: 1670

of primordial floods,

of meteoric showers and falls,

such destruction transporting myriads away,

before ere their thinking collected.

                                            22.17

And for those who suppose

that these their barns,

their wines, their houses,

were by some chance acquired:

it was God alone, who did provide,   1680

all of this our bounty.

22.19

So the pure see this and laugh,

the righteous add these judgements as a sign,

a badge:

"the Divine has the sentence passed:

our enemies are demised!

their crushing by wealth they acquired themselves".

22.21

So crawl, crawl, upon your knees,

1690

beg, beg for mercy,

be at peace with our Lord,

and witness your own increase,

your prosperity returning.

22.22

Accept the words, the laws and these teachings,

guarding them in your inner reaches.

22.23

Thus your returning,

comes in ejecting all your evil motivations,

1700

and the trashing of your money.

22.25

But the 'gold' of your new wealth,

will no longer be felt:

it's the Divine shine on your living,

your valuing of this approving.

22.27

Your prayers,

your praises, will rise to God;

your promises, the Divine reflect,

1710

your word, as good as the act itself.

22.29

Your mere glance

will lift the downtrodden up,

and God will enact your pleas of clemency,

as you direct.

23

23.2   1720

In my bitter complaining,

I risk thoughts of rebellion:

Your hand it rests heavy upon me;

Ignore not my groaning!

Please let me find You,

the place of Your dwelling;

to unfold my cause,

not pausing to inform of its many clauses;

to wait, to hear of Your deciding.

Which way: Your verdict, Your judging?

23.8   1730

O Lord, tell me of Your location!

I've been places and You were not there,

and upon my return still didn't find You;

one says "God is there" but I cannot see it,

"over here", yet I discover no proof.

23.11

Yet me He seems to see and of this I approve,

for should I be tested,

my core will be golden:

these feet have not wavered   1740

and firm is this hold on Your track.

23.12

Lord, your words do not leave me,

o'rewriting my own daily needs;

23.13

you alone O Lord are God alone,

your actions and Being are one;

23.14

to my afflictions you're adding

not one more than my portion;   1750

your presence would freeze me,

your terrors would seize me,

making rigid my bones.

By God I am sapped,

my spirit stripped bear,

and through the Divine alone.

23.17

Still I remain,

and speak to this void overshadowing me.

24   1760

24.1

The liars and frauds,

they live, they work,

so care You not to record their days?

Why give them space to deface our place,

this world you have built for our sharing?

They demolish our heritage,

rip-up communities,

dismemb'ring friend-from-friend.

24.4   1770

Though but like us, in arrogance bully,

they fuss, 'till their way is made smooth,

and that queue is for us, not them.

They care not whose bread they scavenge:

from the poor, the aged or the young,

and of those who remain,

they confine to some ghetto,

some place the rich need not see;

so not seen is their scraping of scraps,

from margins, from bins,

after their masters' repast.

24.7

Likewise for clothing,

they hunt amongst those,

who to merchants can't turn,

freezing and dripping,

'gainst cold and the rain;

some taken for traffic,

in pain and great suff'ring,

stealing from those who have naught,

24.11

forcing crime on such,

who through crime alone,

alive remain.

24.12

Passing alleys at night,

I hear of their plight,

but God dances not to their tune.

24.13

And still, in some others monsters are born,

who rebel and ignore our society,

rejecting those ways we have crafted,

that make for community working;

dark in heart, dark in deed,

murdering in shadows and thieving at night,

24.15

stealing those hearts that aren't theirs to take,

thinking "of what none can see,

none can sense make",

masking their faces of horrors;

disguised by night and hid-up by day,

they think to lie undetected,

(exposure to them and the loss of their name,

like the terrors of death unto others).

24.18

Yet, on the sweeping waters of history,

barely a ripple they make,

their plots un-allotted on earth;

hell as a home, waiting for all those,

who fire on earth inflicted;   1820

24.20

as the ground and its lodgers,

worm through the boxes,

the lodgings for all their corpses.

24.21

The widow, the childless,

the strong and the weak,

all alike in their talents are taken;

24.23

some hedged about, some are forsaken,   1830

but all have their times recorded.

24.24

And all this is true:

so who's to challenge, prove me wrong,

in my contentions?

25

The Bildad the Shuhite answered:

25.2

Power beyond Power,

might beyond Might,   1840

in singleness are of the Lord alone,

giving peace within God's halls on high.

25.3

What are armies to such power,

our might facing Heaven's?

25.4

Can a man be justified before such divinity;

a woman be pure in the sight of its Maker?

25.5

Neither nova nor quasar,   1850

attests such purity through brightness,

25.6

still less the human, who is but worm and dust.

26

Then Job replied:

26.2

Oh what heights of virtue,

to raise the oppressed as you do!

And see how you release those

with no power to set free!   1860

26.3

You are so able to inform us

mere infants in letters,

yet I do wonder of which pure muse,

these your delights do now spring?

26.5

(A hymn to God's power)

Maelstroms: cosmic in extent,

envelope as if from naught,

worlds entire and their peoples,   1870

in motion upset;

prior bastions no longer fortresses seem,

the dead, the sphere of life,

accident and calamity,

all flattened in obeisance be.

Vectors in concept placed,

earth's space: what does it transcribe?

Meteorology:

its secrets hiding in commonplace experience;

and the place of Your dwelling?   1880

Is it here or beyond our highest seeing?

                                                                                    26.10

This home of your manufacture:

you divided night from light,

land and depths,

for a time and times beyond our mere living;

Your stopping, your ceasing of Heaven's playing,

is to us a mystery beyond fathoming;

                                                                                    26.12

and when expressed in the seas arresting,   1890

and in species ending, is revealing of your power.

                                                                                    26.13

Chaos cleared at the Spirit's word

and the evil serpent paid

for his arrogant misleading;

                                                                                  · 26.14

All this, all these are but dimly perceived,

minor revealings of your ways, but faintly,

as in a whisper heard.

We cannot grasp this power beyond Power.   1900

27

Then Job resumes his discourse and says:

                                                                                    27.2

I swear by the Living God,

though I've not seen his justice t'ward me,

and my life is a tragedy,

whilst the Creator's breath sustains me in life,

the Spirit in my consciousness remains,

I will not take evil words in my mouth,

neither the frauds and lies of others inhabit.   1910

You are none of you in the right,

and my rightness I do not lay down;

that my cause is just I can not deny,

still less contemplate its passing by.

27.6

I refuse the voice of my conscience:

I am guiltless, and to say else is lies.

27.7

Thus I identify my enemy as the wicked,

my accusers: 'im-moralisers' them all!   1920

27.8

(The lot of the Godless)

Hope flies when those without God pass on;

why expect deliverance in death,

when in life the Divine is ignored?

27.10

Be abandoned to God's praise,

to be abandoned in God's care!

Let me of the Divine a teacher be,

to instruct you in the Lord's words;   1930

and now abandon idle talk:

take hold of God's truthful ways.

27.13

Thus the sword is fed by the Lord,

off the portion meant for the abuser,

those stealers of our inheritance;

their posterity eaten alive by famine,

by those who thrive on their thieving,

with none mourning their passing,

still less their partners in life.   1940

And their piles of wealth, of clothing, of housing?

The meek, the peacemaker, those righteous:

these will profit from their gambling of life,

their punt that their take on morals,

on the way of Life's living,

was all just meant for their own taking;

so fragile, so weak is their edifice of thinking;

their day, its prosperity, dims,

to be followed by a sorrowful eternity.

It will all be swept away in the flood that is death;   1950

the ripping of money,

of wealth from evil's place;

their name blown away on the derision,

the hissing,

the clapping of those remaining:

them who see but stupidity.

28

Of all humanity's exploring:

there is no end to its depths of uncovering,

yet what is to be found in this work,   1960

this struggling?

28.1

Silver and gold are mined,

Iron and copper from the depths are dug.

By the explorer,

deepest darkness is enlightened;

far dimensions are found and brightened.

Remote and obscure is the place of our aim,

neither eye seen nor ear heard

- indeed no human has been -   1970

to such locations;

there left to themselves,

with no hope of assistance;

'great delvers' satisfy their human existence.

Does matter beyond burning,

reveal great mysteries of being?

Far above our presence, our size, our mere frailties,

knowledge gives vision beyond human framing.

Great moments above and below our earthly placing,

revealing beauties nere thought to be seen.   1980

These our meaning strive, in this revealing,

to bring forth some knowledge,

to set forth our condition,

as ever unsettled,

outreaching this space, this void,

our home, our placing.

                                                    28.12

And yet the question remains:

where wisdom,

where is true understanding?   1990

                                        28.13

Can humanity value,

what is not found in the lands of this living?

The deep fails to reveal its true meaning:

neither sea, space nor earth,

confess to its hiding;

Gold beyond gold fails to balance its price;

neither can silver as substitute for wisdom suffice.

Thus in trying all other items of wealth,

diamonds, skins, minerals and oil   2000

- none can equal in the contest of balance and value,

wisdom itself.

                                        28.20

Where is it sourced, that the hunt be commenced?

It is plain:

wisdom is not in plain sight to beast, bird or person.

28.22

Disaster and death in their avoiding,

give the semblance of wisdom,

28.23   2010

yet only God alone guards it's gates,

and knows of its placing.

28.24

With piercing vision, God sees above,

behind and before all on earth,

and through heaven's heaven.

In the Divine shaping of Creation's shapers,

(the wind and the rain),

the Lord ordered by these their forces,

to have boundaries and paths.   2020

The 'Shaper of shapers', is as Wisdom known:

studied, measured, assessed, discerned,

and in a proverb revealed:

"Reverence the Lord, this is wisdom;

reject evil and yours is its child:

true understanding."

29

29.1

Then Job continued and said:

29.2   2030

Oh that in returning,

I might recreate my time in months past,

when God hovering over,

did guard me,

guide me through dark shades,

and by his light my path did illuminate.

29.4

Then was I in full spate, my life,

my works spilling from my hand,

29.5   2040

when God my hand in friendship did take.

In company surrounded,

my interests and businesses lauded,

fruitful in all my endeavours,

giving me an entrance into palaces and councils

and the awed respect of elders

and the younger fellows,

each severally:

rising to greet me

being silent before me   2050

and standing to hear me

29.11

All this did please me,

affirming, at times blessing.

Enabling my blessing of those who needed me:

the poor, the orphan, those lacking a champion

and in turn, raining upon me,

the well wishing of the dying and the widow.

my alms they clothed me,

like a garment my charity enveloped me,   2060

being an enabler for disability,

and parent to the needy;

and in extending my blessing

became even a magistrate to the stranger,

parrying the violence of the hater

and prising the innocent from the jaws of the monster.

29.18

In payment of which,

I thought me most likely,

to die in my bed,   2070

at peace and in great length of days;

my influence never waining

even at my place of resting,

and my health in fine fettle, even at my passing.

29.21

indeed none at the time passing-up the opportunity

to hear wise words fall from my lips,

their import and authority

silencing all those before me;

my advice being prized 2080

beyond that of good fortune,

money and blessing;

my knowledge confounding those sceptics,

who sought to quash my deep gifting.

29.25

Thus I was as a prince amongst them;

a marshall to their troop.

30

30.1

And now? 2090

now they cast me down in derision;

I am disgusting to them,

those young who once stood in silence waiting,

whose fathers in truth fain would I have employed,

to wash my floors, my halls.

Men? barely that,

so little in fact that they were of little use to me;

mere farmers of patch and briar,

naming desert and scrub as 'acreage',

tillers of dust and straw. 2100

30.5

They're ejected from their communities,

and assumed to be thieves and spongers,

condemned to make house

in places estranged from others,

huddled together in puddles and mud;

30.8

even their names are not mentioned,

not counted, not registered.

30.9   2110

These are they now:

disgusted by me!

that very exemplar of obscene disaster,

they the rejected, reject me now too,

lower than the lowest am I become,

blotter for their spittle and bile.

30.11

Seeing the Divine cutting me loose,

has set them free to cat call,

to beat, to abuse;   2120

before this mob I am driven out,

to run the gauntlet,

to a blind alley of no escaping,

adorned with thorns for my whipping.

They delight, are fuelled,

by this my ripped paining.

30.14

And now, with no hope of a champion,

they are become unrestrainèd in their caning,

their flailing, their piercing,   2130

of my boundary, this body, my framing.

30.15

I am become a magnet for their terrors:

prosperity, honour and name pursued,

have fled.

30.16

And so my motivation destroyed,

day-after-day this suffering confines me;

night follows night of His gnawing my bones;

30.19   2140

with my clothing he strangles me,

casting me into the mud,

chewing on dust and ashes.

I'm screaming for help,

yet as to one deaf.

Should I stand: you spin me about to face you.

I feel your cruelty now, and the blows of your hand,

as in a storm I am buffeted,

tossed-up and dismembered.

30.23   2150

I know now I am presented to death,

the end of all who draw breath.

30.24

Yet why beat one who is down?

Who both lifted the down-trodden

and wept for the battered?

30.26

I trusted for good, but darkness appeared;

when light was expected, disaster erupted.

30.27   2160

This heart, my motor,

is starved, compressed, constricted;

even my breathing,

screeches from pain-to-pain,

confronting my hours, 'till - when?

30.28

The councillors in those assemblies,

would fain entertain me,

now I am burnt brown and smelly to them.

30.29   2170

The bat, the hedgehog, the deer,

- one feral as me -

now my sole friends appear to be.

30.30

My sun-stroke in one season,

is cold fever in another;

my music, no cheer can bring.

31

31.1

2180

Of what am I accused?

Did I harbour thoughts

towards one not mine to hold,

though I vowed to keep my passions on hold,

for my covenanted one?

Yet I am assured

of the Lord's judgement 'gainst those,

whose flesh contends with the Almighty.

The Lord must surely record all my actions?

If I have erred, have sinned,

will He not judge with justice,

2190

decide rightly,

in tipping the scales t'wards me,

who has not veered from His path?

31.7

Had I in stupidity gone after another's,

or one not mine to take,

had stinked my hands with a bribe,

had been 'on the make',

then let another,

all that is mine appropriate.

2200

31.9

And so I assert again:

if that had been my crime,

or I had with violence

entertained murderous thoughts toward my neighbour,

31.10

then let her who is my spouse,

espouse her soul to another,

taking his name, his house,

his wares, his fame,   2210

31.11

for this would be a shame,

a crime,

and in disgust I should be unmasked,

as the villain I am.

31.12

Such fractioning of promises for time given,

is a consumption, a tempest,

a conflagration,

that would consume all that's to my name;   2220

31.13

and for another:

if I have abhorred those

who to my house

have covenanted their souls,

the wealth of their labour,

and in dispute, in power,

favoured myself over them,

I could not my Lord face,

to the Divine,   2230

my case make.

31.15

For, of this we are all convinced,

(though in tragedy veil such truth to ourselves),

our Lord did us both make!

And thus should I refuse my hand

to those whom the Creator for a time

might cause somewhat less to hold,

to have, to make:

I am become to them as the Snake, 2240

one who would not split his take,

with those who had none.

31.18

Yet to me, this is not the verity!

For from my earliest years,

my time, my wealth,

I have deployed in benefit:

to the parentless, as a parent;

to those lacking a mate,

as greater than a friend; 2250

to those lacking a covering, as clothing;

or to those lacking warmth, heat.

31.20

Indeed even those who lacked thanks,

did not find my blessing of them lacking.

31.21

Should one uncover me having privily

cast my lot in court unrighteously

'gainst those who had naught,

then rightly let me suffer loss, 2260

my limbs falling from their sockets!

31.23

For nere did I treat the Lord's tolerance lightly,

His mercies did always terrify me,

for fear they meant I had erred,

against Divinity's majesty.

If I have ever trusted in my wealth as security,

let that be to me as stupidity.

31.26

Indeed if I have ever imagined against my Lord, 2270

some other as God;

if ever declared: knowledge, fame, power,

anything like as unto Divinity the same,

then let me be condemned,

and false unto my Lord declaimed.

31.29

Please God that I did never rejoice

over mine enemy's calamity,

or a party throw 'cause of his misadventure;

nor seek a curse upon his head,   2280

and so sin against their personhood;

31.31

neither do I seek my retainers,

to fight by proxy on my behalf,

'specially should my supplièd goods,

be below parity.

31.32

I want no visitor, no stranger,

to pass me by when lacking bedding,

or a covering against the night;   2290

neither do I want such an allegation,

still less the fact, that in covering,

in robbing transparency,

I hid, I obscured the truth,

and justice did thwart

(even if encouraging,

the mob were baying with their kin,

at my gate).

31.35

But I speak to the wind!   2300

And there is no one hearing me.

I have now made my mark,

my case I have staked;

let the Almighty hear me and answer!

Oh that I had some charge, some sheet,

I could check, me would excuse.

Such a paper I would count a monument,

for in its refutation,

it would become unto me a crown,

and an accounting of my ways,   2310

my steps.

31.38

For I know the very ground in my possession,

would become to me an oppressive force,

a curse,

should I have robbed any of payment

for supplies I used in its producing of plenty,

of bounty;

instead of crops

some poisoned weeds would appear.   2320

The words of Job are ended.

32

32.1-5

So these three men ceased to answer Job, because he was righteous in his own eyes. Then the wrath of Elihu the son of Barachel the Buzite, of the family of Ram, was kindled against Job. His wrath was kindled because he justified himself rather than God. Also his wrath was kindled against Job's three friends, because they had found no answer, and yet had condemned Job. Now Elihu had waited to speak to Job, because they were older than he. When Elihu saw that there was no answer from these three, his anger grew.   2330

32.6

Elihu spoke out and said:

I am a youth, you are elders;

I was shy; I was afraid to speak;

Should not wisdom talk?

I thought those of an age should speak.

But then: God's Spirit inspiration provides.

Some older ones have it, others are lacking.

So too with justice:

some possessing it, others omitting. 2340

Thus I say,

"Listen to me.

I too will tell you of my thinking."

32.11

I waited for your words;

when they came,

I dissected your case,

your scrabbling about for some sense.

And so did notice,

that none of you 2350

did once call time on Job's statements.

So it's wrong to suggest,

that you have found some great chest,

or even vestige of, wisdom.

It is to God alone we must turn,

for any refutation of his clauses.

His marshalling being not against me,

I shan't arraign your words against his.

32.15

Indeed mere words have failed all three, 2360

and consequently, they are refuted.

32.16

Your pausing is gnawing at me:

should I delay on account of your being confounded?

32.17

No: though young I will give of my tongue,

let them have of my opinion,

of my experience, my times.

Weight of words is mine, yet reverence slows me;

as some new buck vigour is with me, 2370

but it is enthusiasm: this risks bettering me!

My vent will blow,

and my pressure relieve,

respecting no title,

giving no bow,

else with such prejudice my Maker would suck,

these my words from me.

33

So now Job, to my speech give ear,

to every detail I mention,

for now I give vent,

have resolved to impart,

my thoughts in uprightness of heart.

So you may be assured of my sincerity:

I assert that I bear of the Spirit's mark,

the Almighty my Maker be.

Thus reply if you can,

and take your stand in this court of ideas.   2390

We are all of God's making,

you and I thus far are alike;

you should therefore these my words embrace,

and in their face,

display no fear.

33.8

I have heard you state,

in my hearing affirm,

that you are pure and without fault,

and clean, having no iniquity.   2400

33.10

And yet you observe that God sees in you an enemy,

shackling you, tracking your ways, your paths.

But this is untrue!

Of the Divinity such must not be said.

Greater than all, our Lord is not fought,

nor expected to answer our calls;

God's calling:

in one manner now, and in another later;

at times heard, and at others never.   2410

For one in a dream, for another their neighbour;

gives words of instruction, of compassion,

of terror;

I purpose to pull away from sin,

from pride,

sparing that person,

from fraud, from lies,

from crossing the River.

                                                  33.19

Others again, are sent some disease,   2420

some affliction, hating their very food,

the wasting of their person, their bodies shrinking,

revealing their bones, this their scaffolding;

                                                  33.22

inviting the fear that it will not cease,

'till death claims this victim.

Yet perchance, there is from God a champion,

who mediates on her behalf,

one in a thousand, who might declare her righteous,

declaiming on her behalf: 2430

"Saved! Saved from destruction, this one:

redeemed from Hells' hole!"

Then would her body,

be re-manufactured,

to that of her youth.

                                          32.26

She would God entreat,

finding delight in Divinity,

whose face she would see,

restoring her wholeness in God.   2440

33.27

Happiness would descend in verse,

whose lyric would be,

"Though I had sinned, insulted my Lord,

done what was wrong, yet my sentence,

was light in comparison.

My being once forfeit, from hell is saved:

light floods my life once again!"

33.29

2450

This is God's way:

not one, but so many, savings are forged,

each undoing Hell's curse,

with light replacing the darkness of death.

33.31

So Job hear and attend!

listen! I speak, take note.

Now reply, that your justice might shout!

But saving that, keep silence,

and I will more wisdom impart.

34

2460

Elihu continues:

Come now all you with wisdom,

you clever who say you know;

34.3

speech invites testing,

as food does its tasting;

let us reason, decide what is right,

establish between us some laws.

34.5

2470

This one Job declares himself faultless,

whilst thinking his case overturned:

34.6

"Why should I lie in my brief?

True, I am pierced,

but am free of any fault;

unfairly accused!"

34.7

See now this Job!

how he piles blasphemies against his God,

34.8   2480

in league with the same,

cavorting with those who frame evil deeds;

34.9

who assert that friendship with God

pays no dividends.

34.10

To those who claim wisdom,

know this: God knows no wickedness,

neither evil performs,

but pays those back their deeds,   2490

their ways folding back on themselves.

Save thoughts of such being unjust!

Divinity does not rule this earth in trust for another!

Were the Lord to give thought to vengeance,

all flesh would be consumed

and return to mere dust.

34.16

So listen, consider,

those who have knowledge,

the power to deploy understanding: 2500

would it seems likely

that Injustice could Justice deploy,

the Impure, Purity condemn?

The Lord puts kings in their place,

nobility knows God's tongue too;

partiality or favour,

to either the poor or the favoured:

these are alien thoughts,

to the One full righteous alone.

All alike the Creator's mark: we bear.   2510

All are the work of God's hands.

                                              34.21

If so with those who rule here below,

what of the Lord above?

What do you suppose?

There is a record stored of all our walking,

our ways,

whether deep below or in the public gaze.

None who forge evil whether in caves or the light,

can expect any flight, from any court,   2520

God might interpose

(though in truth,

there is but slight chance

such would precede

swift judgement on the mighty,

indeed on any who commit deeds of iniquity).

                                              34.25

"And so to bed"; yet they do not rise,

these mighty from their lying, their frauds,

and are instead overtaken in their repose.   2530

Others are visited in the public space,

crushed, their crimes pasted-up for all to see,

disgraced for facing away from the Divinity

and having no regard for the Lord's ways and laws.

The entreaties of those they had crushed:

the poor, the diseased, those afflicted

were laid before the Lord,

and in a folding motion,

crushed those who had at the first them launched.

                                        34.29   2540

And if instead there's silence from the Throne:

what then?

No hymn can entreat the Lord

to reframe those choices made,

still less for us to ring the bell and see the Face,

to make Divinity accountable;

whether a person, people or a nation;

so that none godless might ensnare, entrap or rule;

neither singly or in multiplicity.

34.31   2550

Neither a wager nor a contract will God accept:

if guilty there is no recompense,

save that which is served, is kept on hand.

So tell us Job! What is your view,

your intelligence?!

But perhaps we should return instead to the wise,

the clever,

who persist in their maintaining

that this Job speaks but vapidly,

and as such   2560

should be judged and condemned limitlessly;

for there is the evil of treason in his sin:

reaping it's canker'd harvest of words

against the Divinity.

35

Elihu continued saying:

35.2

And so to your views.

Do tell, this from you:

"I set my right before Yours"   2570

Is this your justice then true?

or again:

"What's sin worth, that of it You take note?

Where is the gain to me

whether iniquity I cause or not?"

To the which I reply, both to you and these 'friends':

stand in awe and take note,

see the clouds, nay the heavens above,

all remote, far above You and I;

this your sinning cannot touch the Lord;   2580

iniquity can never dent Divinity!

Neither is your goodness currency to God.

                                                    35.8

Both your evil and your right deeds

impinge on you alone.

Indeed, corruption and oppression

have their own voice and with it

invoice their debt of right to God,

calling for the Lord's might

to slam against those mighty,   2590

who thieve their rights from them;

                                                    35.10

Why, when we enquire of the void,

"Where is the Creator God?",

(who raises us alone to the artistry of Art

and leaves none for the brute beasts below),

do we hear no reply?

The Lord for sure will not an answer intone

to us prideful souls

(those whose acts dilute to disappear,   2600

their words of woe).

And so Job consider:

why should God listen

when you the Divinity ignore?

And is not God's deafness

a symptom of rage

at the multiplication of your wordy vapidity?

36

Elihu continued saying:

36.2   2610

Stay now yet a while longer,

tarry for further instruction,

for on God's side I have yet further words to offer;

As is my wisdom so is God's charge:

full rounded and with justice riven;

As is my purity so is God's power:

complete and without side;

I am in words truth

to God's brave-heart of action,

36.6   2620

who ends the lives of the wicked

whilst returning the poor to their livings;

36.7

Thus Justice exalts these our nation's icons:

both the right living and the ruler alike.

36.8

Yet should the tables be turned

and imprisonment earned,

with the icon stamped in the dust,

God is on-hand to reveal pride as the band,   2630

which threatens to tighten the noose.

And so the veil from the eye is removed,

a correcting of ways,

leading to pleasantness and prosperity.

But of the reverse!?

Should you refuse such correction

be prepared the River to face,

to cross over

and extinction to taste.   2640

36.13

Rage and anger

are food for these

who refuse to know God,

where discipline leads to no turning.

36.14

They die in their youth,

disgorged on their own profanities.

Yet those turned by correction,

see God's face through their suffering,   2650

being plucked from the mouth of Destruction,

then emptied into wide restful spaces,

with comfort and food abiding.

36.17

But now consider the first:

corralled by justice and judgement,

take care lest like them,

you are taken by wealth and enticements.

36.19

Would your gold serve to uphold you,   2660

purge all pain from your life?

Could your might truly work wonders?

Do not trust in fables of fairies,

dragging your enemies hence!

36.21

And feast not on darkness as a sop for your terrors,

 - your testing being done for a reason -

such trials are your teachers,

taught by our Master;

there being not one like our Lord;   2670

whom no arm does guide or judge rightly.

So forever recall God's praises to tell,

the Lord's works to proclaim on the stage;

for all humanity

can only but stand in awe,

gazing upon such majesty,

written in Creation's patterning.

36.26

Thus we know God is great,

beyond our imagining, 2680

with a lifetime unending,

sustaining the earth, its crops,

-our sustaining-

by water: liquid, solid, evaporating,

then precipitating to cycle around once again.

Such an abundance: who can grasp it?

Weather in wind and rain and thunder,

crashing against our vision,

like great bolts hurled across the oceans;

Such an abundance, 2690

supplying our food, our bounty.

Divinity with mighty power:

awed we cower,

both reminded and rewarded;

savanna's beasts

heralding the great storm's approaching.

37

Cowering and trembling,

its anchors shaking,

my heart precesses my chest; 2700

arresting my ears

on the sound of God's thunder,

the roaring of Divinity's voice;

there's no place that's deaf to its clamours,

sheer power envelopes our thought.

Comprehension is deaf to God's wonders:

the bright white of pure snow,

he soft touch of rain

and

he beating drum of the storm   2710

All such events

arresting our actions,

entailing our thoughts as to "why?".

All the beasts of the field,

as heralds of God,

have the sense to take shelter in fear.

                                                                37.9

Winds from the north,

race meeting air from the south,

and in embracing menace,   2720

great spirals create.

                                                                37.10

Cold blasting air freezes water in shards,

to shoot daggers glittering past;

and where it meets pools,

their contents it cools,

to form fine mirrors and paths.

                                                                37.11

And damp feeds the clouds,

'till engorged they explode   2730

in the bright blue of the lightening;

                                                                37.12

the which seems forever to be requesting directions,

crashing from heaven to heaven,

at times touching earth,

in correction or impression,

all sourced in the grandeur of God.

37.14

To whom you O Job in paying attention,

should be revelling in this evidencing of greatness, 2740

for we, none of us, can explain how God,

entails the heavens to show us their revels:

the lightening flashing,

the storm's gathering,

the building of the clouds;

these wonders have their source,

in perfection of knowledge;

37.17

the which moderates or intensifies

Creation's energies in ways unknown; 2750

moulding the skies in varying guises,

at times leaden,

and at time brazen.

37.19

All is to our interpretation,

like thick smoke to intelligence;

should we enquire,

surely we would be swallowed alive

for the impertinence of questioning our Lord?

O such brilliance, 2760

hidden as is the sun's core,

entrapped in its brightness upon a cloudless day.

Might such not herald God's arrival in aural splendour?

Who can compare with such majesty?

37.23

God the Lord: to you we do not hold our candle;

Power beyond power

yet gentle in raising justice and right-living.

O nations, do you not fear the Lord,

who has no rapport 2770

with them who hold

themselves above this One?

38

The Lord answered Job out of the raging storm and replied:

38.2

Who is this pushing-out words saving context,

demeaning knowledge in the breadth of their paucity?

Look yourself in the mirror!

Who are you?

Take hold! 2780

I'll ask - you answer:

Were you there:

when I laid out the laws that frame your framing?

Were you there?

Give of your understanding!

And of these laws:

what of their terms, their enumerations?

Were you there?

And of the substance,

the energy of Creation's placing, 2790

of its framing;

were you there?

Of the heavens,

their locales of radiation:

the star's companions,

clouds and quasars:

when these in rapturous blazing,

exploded praise for their creating;

Were you there?

And of those in my court 2800

who lauded these detonations in revels and exultation;

were you there?

38.8

And of the place of human placing,

this earth, this orb,

this blessed womb of your unfolding:

of it and its magic,

those boundaries of context, of living:

of sea, ocean and shore,

of female and male,   2810

yet forth from one core;

of the naked energy of our living space:

this land, our rain, our breezes, our storms;

to all of these are limits set:

of times, of breadth,

of soulful impact and import;

                                                                                    38.11

to this mark your move is made,

beyond this you have no authority,

no haunt, no meaning for your existing.   2820

                                                                                    38.12

Thus where is your power?

Can you configure the sun as it rises?

Of the dawn: in all its myriad processes?

(One being the uncovering of dark dealings of night,

                                                                                    38.14

the rising light raising surfaces from the schemering,

                                                                                    38.15

snuffing evil's power and breaking its expectant victory).

                                                                   38.16   2830

Of the endless seas:

where is their source?

Have you resourced such abundant plenty?

Are these heaven-formed or of the deep?

What would you know?!

And what of the limit to your term:

have you seen the clocks,

for each a ticking of one's span of years?

38.18

And of those places as yet unseen,

2840

what of these?

Does your conscious mind of such behold?

38.19

Of the good and of the bad:

can you name the source of either?

And of their limits and their borders:

can you describe their hoarders and their despisers?

38.21

And since quite plainly you were observing:

describe the snows and their manufacture,

2850

the origins of the hail,

where used in war and battle.

Reveal the framing of such laws of hailings,

since you were present at their writing!

And again: what of the lightenings and their erupting?

The great storming winds and their rendings?

38.25

And so to the travels of phenomena:

are they there where no eye does see them:

countering the drought, making deserts rich,

2860

fertile places once again?

38.28

Can you a father to the rain be,

or of its little twin, the dew?

38.29

Are you indeed the Great Congealer,

birthing glaciers and sharp frosts alike?

38.31

Do you play the filaments

orchestrating movements of great constellations,

2870

being to them any one of the four seasons,

each in its succession?

38.32

Are you the conductor of their manuscripts,

being maestro to both stars and the planets?

38.34

Do you command Earth's daily ablutions

with but a casual bleary word,

38.35

or brief the bolts at their waking,   2880

calling rolling calls in heavenly assemblies?

or perchance my enquiries are too ethereal:

what of the closer 'sophistry':

is it to you wisdom or a lie?

If the first: command the clouds to rain from on high,

turning dust into a traveller's quagmire.

38.39

Do you wonder how the lioness is fed?

Do you place food in endless chains

that ultimately in balance   2890

satisfy every rung of nature's alimentary stairs?

38.41

Or what of the countless chicks,

perched precariously twixed life and death,

in hedge, thicket or upon rocky ledges:

what of their hourly cries:

do they impinge upon your ears or mine?

39

39.1

The ibex or the deer far from here with none to assist: 2900

give birth after … what, what time period?

And their young,

living in the open,

thrive,

soon to disappear to start the cycle in their turn once again;

likewise the great fauna,

solitary in their several haunts,

make desolations into fruitful habitations;

estranged from civil society,

preferring their own company to that of tamer or driver;   2910

and will judge you the unwelcome guest at their feast of rough tubers and stubby leaves;

rudely ignoring your offers of servanthood or slavery in the service of humanity;

can you through any expended energies,

invite these celebrations of wilderness and tenacity

to follow after you in loosing their liberty?

                                                        39.13

Of parents in the wilderness:

there are many nurturing the regeneration in cycles of their own species;

but give your reasoning for the success of these examples that neither wait nor   2920
care:

like the ostrich or the turtle;

each has talents unmatched by others,

yet merely covers their young,

unconcerned some scavenger might happen there upon,

or another might in resting crush the same.

Far less nurture,

some will consume their progeny,

as if in demonstration of their lacking sense,

of the uselessness of their labours.   2930

And what of those beasts

who far outstrip the human

in speed, sight or abilities of smell?

Were you the forger of such paragons

of beauty or complexity?

In ever finer detail,

greater mystery lies;

in ever greater spaces.

Your mendacity can escue

such wonders as are evidently before your sensing.   2940

And from that pattern and rigid conformity

to the rules set by Divinity.

Your face can turn away,

carving provenance from nothings to nothings,

which is an impossibility.

Thus you look for sense and reasonings,

upon a stage set by your own musing history,

rejecting My majesty,

evidenced in Creation's beauteous creativity.

40   2950

Then the Lord said to Job:

                                                                40.2

Contender?!

Show yourself; who would contend with me!

Are you attempting correction?

Give of an answer!

                                                                40.4

(But Job, rightly discerning his depravity,

stopped his mouth, his words,

proclaiming himself unworthy: 2960

                                                                40.5

"Once I tried, even twice-over I attempted,

but now repent:

my paucity registered.")

                                                                40.6

Then the Lord answered Job out of the raging storm:

                                                                40.7

Take hold of yourself:

prepare for this exam.

I pose the questions 2970

and to you I turn for the answer:

40.8

In inverting my laws,

would you turn my righteousness into yours,

shifting guilt to balance the equation?

40.9

Does your reach compare with Mine,

your arm enact your commanding words:

40.10

Then let me see your cloth and gold, 2980

such splendour to arrest,

to hold your courtiers in your halls,

40.11

or demonstrate in spilling wrath and anger,

your justice wreaked upon the proud,

those hunters of the poor.

40.14

Such visions of such your might,

might cause me to re-think my judgements

and judge you capable, 2990

of saving grace to you-ward at the least.

40.15

Yet of grace towards creativity?

Creation's gilding of mechanism,

exploding effusions, of blessing, in fecundity?

Of these, humanity in flesh is of a like,

Though these consume not meat,

yet as meat are consumed by you.

See here and appreciate the power in blessing,

in overwhelming multiplicity of bounty, 3000

each species severally taking of its place,

a niche,

and in that location,

making play as king, ruling its plenty.

Some in plain,

some of mountain,

some in vents of oceans deep,

concealèd and in secret,

yet reproductively all succeed,

as befits my effusive creativity,   3010

of blessed fecundity.

41

Will your fears be landed with a mere fisher's hook?

What of your barbs:

do these tame such beastly terrors?

Could you loop or lasso your frozen moments,

whipping yourself free from any accident and calamity?

Predations are in audacious ventures lurking:

who grants way-leave to captains or explorers?

Can you gift what you cannot control,   3020

or assumptions make of that beyond your remit?

Is hope exploring fallacious territory

and audacious pride consuming rationality?

Will your hand return from touching such ferocity

or your timidity touch reason and gift you your longevity?

Who has played beyond their shell,

trusting my forbearance,

accepting that I hold it all in its existence?

Thus I will not keep silence

in considering such blessings of your peace: 3030 my gifts to you of this home, this orb,

an happy sanctuary from celestial tempest,

from all-consuming energies;

you are in my sheltering sheltered and at peace,

for you and none of yours can bulwarks make

'gainst such terrors as you can but image telescopically,

sheltered by time and distance,

from destructions unimaginable.

There is no conscience in such might!

It will not consult with you, your rights to life,   3040

to home, to family.

And kid not yourself

that humanity has some nobility

when facing such ferocity:

it does not know,

you it can not fear;

its magnificence is raw;

it's might: white sheets of expanding raucous multiplying shelled energies;

nothing here can prepare you for such sights.

Why is it there?   3050

Why is it not here?

Do not in arrogance assumptions create,

for that of which your context,

no sense can make.

42

[Job's reply]

Of nothing I know anything,

save that you Oh Lord know all,

and of this all

have given so much to us.   3060

Of none of your deciding,

does any come to naught.

In answer to your asking:

"who aired words saving context,

demeaning very knowledge",

it t'was I,

I who spoke of what I do not know.

Right graciously you Oh Lord,

kindly did engage with me, so lacking wisdom,

declaring that you would speak and that I should pay attention.   3070

                                                                                            42.5

In times past I knew of you, but by rumour only,

yet now you have appeared to me,

speaking as like unto a neighbour.

I despise myself,

knowing me far beneath all measure.

Epilogue 42.7

It was so, that after God had spoken these words to Job, God said to Eliphaz the
Temanite, "My wrath is kindled against you, and against your two friends; for you
have not spoken of me the thing that is right, as my servant Job has. Now   3080
therefore, take to yourselves seven bulls and seven rams, and go to my servant
Job, and offer up for yourselves a burnt offering; and my servant Job shall pray
for you, for I will accept him, that I not deal with you according to your folly. For
you have not spoken of me the thing that is right, as my servant Job has."

So Eliphaz the Temanite and Bildad the Shuhite and Zophar the Naamathite
went, and did what God had commanded them, and God accepted Job.

God overturned the captivity of Job, once he had prayed for his friends.

God gave Job twice as much as he had before. Then came there to him all his
brothers, and all his sisters, and all those who had been of his acquaintance
before, and ate bread with him in his house. They comforted him, and consoled   3090
him concerning all the evil that God had brought on him. Everyone also gave him

piece of money, and everyone a ring of gold.

o God blessed the latter end of Job more than his beginning. He had fourteen
housand sheep, six thousand camels, one thousand yoke of oxen, and a
housand female donkeys. He had also seven sons and three daughters. He
alled the name of the first, Jemimah; and the name of the second, Keziah; and
he name of the third, Keren Happuch. In all the land were no women found so
eautiful as the daughters of Job. Their father gave them an inheritance among
heir brothers.

After this Job lived one hundred forty years, and saw his sons, and his sons'   3100
ons, to four generations. So Job died, being old and full of days.

notes/overall

1.

Many readers might expect writings to be structured with a beginning, middle and an end. It confirms the picture of our larger world view. Yet not all biblical writings are fitted together in this way. Famously the book of Leviticus has in the past been thought of as being "all over the place" in terms of structure. A proposed 'ring' structure has not found universal acceptance in-spite of one of the greatest of the modern commentators on that book believing towards the end of his life, that it did have one. Ecclesiastes is it seems constructed on a plan predicated on some numerical value of its key word.

3110

In the case of Job the explanations for the apparent transposition of various blocks of text, each obscure in meaning themselves, is often thought to be the result of errors in copying. Perhaps they were, although my own experience of copying-out large volumes of text, tells me that yes indeed I may put text in the wrong place, but I notice it very soon too and have done so *in every case*: after only a few words you realise what it is you are doing. Thus I am not convinced by the explanation that such inconsistencies - involving, it must be said quite large chunks of text in chapters 25 to 28 and elsewhere - are caused by copyists' errors. Instead I wonder if there is another structure to this book, beyond the obvious one.

3120

For this reason I have chosen to leave the apparently misplaced blocks where they occur in the received text, knowing full well that the reader is more than capable of reading each block of text for what it is.

2.

As has been already said, there are many places in Job where both the language and its meaning are obscure. In these cases commentators have referred to other ancient translations of the book in an attempt to gain some clarity. Certainly that is one tool that might be used to aid elucidation. However an other is to consider where else in Job or in the bible as a whole, similar word patterns or thoughts might be expressed. Such an aide is predicated upon the view that the same God inspired all of the writings or again if that is unacceptable, that those who were writing would think it apposite to consult other writings in their tradition

3130

before penning their own, in order that what they wrote might be   3140
seen as part of a wider indeed even cultural, understanding. I have
attempted at times, and in considering other commentators' views
on a particular difficult text, to employ this second method, and such
will then inform this verse presentation.

In this way I have taken Psalms 38 and 77 to be particularly
pertinent, as expressing in compact form that which is written and
explored in greater depth, throughout the whole of Job. Moreover in
terms of the *telos* of the work as a whole, I have taken Psalm 73 as
my model: a journey into God revealing God-self in a deeply
personal manner to the enquirer.   3150

A key concept in Job is that of 'justification': Job wishes to explain
himself to whomever might be listening effectually. At first Job
addresses his explanations to his friends or comforters. These latter
are effectively the guardians of his reputation in the wider
community. Finding these persosn wanting, Job moves the focus of
his attempts increasingly towards God. The tipping-point or turning
for this, I would suggest, occurs in chapter 23, where Job now starts
to turn away from these so-called friends and in addition to seeking
God for justification, seeks God as an objective or person in God-
self. I acknowledge that this turning is only gradual and indeed only   3160
finds its fullest expression in ch 42.5. Yet it is there nonetheless.
Thus I perceive the text of Job to describe a journey of and in faith:
from the position where an honest and true person (man or woman)
who does right yet only as a moral objective owned by themselves,
is transformed through suffering to know the reason why that
morality that they followed, is there at all. In discovering that
'reason' they encounter God as a living person. It is God who in
revealing of God-self's person, ultimately transforms Job.

3.

Overall the motivator in this and indeed other similar works I have   3170
undertaken, is to ask, "If the writer were doing so now, what would
they write?". The effect of this consideration is broadly two-fold in
that it both allows me wide scope in what I put down and yet in the
context of translation or paraphrase or even of parody, does not
permit me to allege fidelity to the text such that I might call it a
translation. Yet a translation is forever available to the reader
whereas an accessible impression of what the meaning might be, is
less so. (Quite plainly 'meaning' in this context is an extraordinary
loaded term and there is no place to explore that here).

The reader is reminded that the text above has markers which enable the paraphrase to be located back into the standard late-medieval versification as seen in modern translations.

notes/7

7.2: there is one or a 'something' that is making him work and toil; but this authority has no interest in him and so in passing doesn't bother to pause and take-in his suffering but neither does it let him be released from it.

The drowning is not in drink but in the tears and endless suffering: there is something terrifyingly banal about it;

notes/16 & 17

3190

References to physical abuse and assault in Job 16.10 and 17.6 would appear to have their answer or solution in Isaiah 50.6.

17.16: a question as to whether hope can survive death itself.

notes/21 & 22

21.8 Following a suggestion by Robert Alter and in view of the fact that this verse reminds us of a verse from the psalms, I have sought to do something similar but with entirely different material. Thus the original uses familiar biblical words to imply sarcastically that Job's comforters are affirming the actuality of such words whilst Job is mocking their understanding in the using of them, on account of his own experience. I could have used any number of such allusions admittedly but I chose, again on account of my own experience (and thus valid in this context), the common thought that the law is there for everybody regardless of status. I use this intentionally in a sarcastic manner.

3200

The reader will notice how the complaints of Job in chapter 21 are echoed by the retort in 22. Job in 21 contends that the evil prosper, whereas in 22 we are told that this is impossible and that they are punished by God, with the punishment itself proving the existence of evil.

3210

notes/23

23.3

Job seeks to find God.

23.13, 14. I view these verses as supportive of that concept known as 'Divine simplicity'.

notes/24

vv 18-25 This is frequently acknowledged to be one of the most obscure in all of Job. Some commentators believe it to be in the wrong place. My rendition assumes that it is in the correct place and forms a development of the sentiments Job has started to express against those who perpetrate evil more generically, (starting in chapter 21 and continuing in 22), as opposed to those expressed against his 'friends', of whom he has long been critical.

3220

notes/28

Here the writer talks about humanity's exploring to great depth and to remotest places but that the thing that is of real value, wisdom, is not found there. We must move into the metaphysical to find wisdom. Thus this chapter is a great exposition of the presence of the transcendent in existence.

notes/30

3230

This chapter marks a change in Job's character, for up to now he has been attacking those who wrongly accused him, successively ever more strongly. Yet here he is starting to attack people out of shear nastiness. This is entirely understandable and I feel the account would have been incomplete without it, since we all, when increasingly hurt and upset, lash out unreasonably.

notes/32-37

Some general remarks on the Elihu speeches: chapter 32 to the end of 37.

Commentators frequently remark on the difficulties associated with this sequence in Job. Having earlier noted that the poetry of the 'comforters' is not as elaborately unique as that of Job himself, several go on to say that the text of the Elihu speeches is an interruption. The text of the comforters' poetry is deemed to have

3240

been shaped to reflect their lack of empathy and nuance in Job's situation. In the case of Elihu it is stated that the flow of the overall book of Job might well have moved from the end of 31 to the start of God's reply at the beginning of 38, omitting Elihu entirely, and no one would have been the wiser or suggested that the Elihu series of speeches, were lost to the text.

3250

The Elihu speeches are deemed to be an interruption because they are variously of lesser poetic quality than that of the other speeches in the book, contain a larger number of Aramaisms, and make use of unique words not used elsewhere in Job. Yet it is plain that the contention of the book is that the Elihu speeches were written by a younger person, at a time in the history of Israel when perhaps Aramaic was transplanting Hebrew as the *lingua franca* of its day, amongst the general population. How would a younger person speak? I submit in a manner that was less polished than his or her older contemporaries; in the 'street speech' of the day and perhaps even, going on our current experience of engaging with the young, making use of words not used by the remainder of the population. They are also more 'black and white' to Job's extreme nuance, didactic to the 'comforters' multiply discursive styles; perhaps at times 'preachy' or even 'shouty' - again, something many of us would expect to find amongst the confident and articulate young of today, and not necessarily any the less truthful or appropriate for that, either. These are the words of just such a younger person and the typography of the utilised poetry reflects this, I would suggest intentionally. I have likewise attempted to reflect this in my own rendering of Elihu's sentiments.

3260

3270

And yet some apparent difficulties remain. Elihu's full name is perhaps when translated less than complimentary about his character. It speaks of his scornfulness: is it a made-up name? Quite possibly, but no less valid and in that sense 'real' for that: this is after all how he is speaking. Elihu is not mentioned anywhere else in the text: the speeches appear and he is no more referred to. He is not condemned or redeemed at the end of the book. Some commentators have suggested that a later 'inserter' of text simply did so with the independently developed Elihu text and then did not see fit to weave Elihu into the frame story. Why ever not, unless this was the intention? The frame stories are hardly complex parts of the overall text should they have required later editing to include detail about Elihu. No indeed, the Elihu speeches I would suggest, are precisely how the words of a younger person are expected to be framed and expected to be placed, within the overall frame of the book.

3280

However and in addition, the Elihu speeches develop the overall theological argument in Job. There are also some further Christological inferences made here.

notes/34

Let the reader note how there is a mirroring of ideas across this chapter where the concepts fronted at the start are then re-visited towards the end.

notes/38

It is common amongst commentators to state that God provides in these magnificent speeches, no answer for Job. I would contend that this assertion is false.

Those in the contemporary IT and science communities will be familiar with the concept of the 'category error', where the lack of comprehension and appreciation of context is such that further, or even a start to an, education is required before meaningful questions or enquiries might then be made.

Thus Job is being answered in the most explicit manner possible and indeed commensurate with his knowledge: 'you have made a category error'. From personal experience, to have made that discovery alone is often of more use than any detailed and systematic explanation, which would in any case be largely unintelligible unless and until the conceptual leap had been made.

notes/39

It is at this stage in the enterprise that I start to depart somewhat more from the descriptive elements of the original. Thus here, where the original speaks of the wondrous power of the horse, I judge that such wonder is not - or rarely - current amongst any of the contemporary readers of this text. I estimate that the reason these comparisons and statements are in the original text is so as to cause a wondrous appreciation of the strength, the monstrous power, of the horse in battle. It is an image that would have occasioned wonder amongst the people of the day. What might work for readers today? Whilst I might have this wrong, I have gone somewhere else to hopefully achieve something of the same.

notes/on chapters 40 and 41

In these final sections of the book of Job, the focus moves from defining the nature of the category error spoken of above, to a challenge to Job himself: thus perhaps something akin to, "this is how the world truly is and now I will question you in the context of this newly revealed reality".

The issue that is being worked upon in chapters 40 and 41 is that God having identified the error to the human (Job), God could then leave Himself open to being challenged. In the Garden of Eden, Adam and Eve at the first did not understand the nature of good and evil; they were not meant to, it was not good for them to know. Take note of the sequence in Genesis 3: it is in two stages, there is the gaining of knowledge (of 'good and evil') and the attempt or the aim, to become like God. In our fallen state, we know about good and evil but have become unable to do much about it. In Jesus we are gifted to become like him and so have been given of the fruit of the 'tree of life' so that we might 'live forever' (Genesis 3.22).   3330

This sequence is now mapped-out in Job as well. Having gained the knowledge of his category error, Job must not now be left to challenge God in his - Job's - newly-found knowledge. That would be a state worst than the first, after all Adam and Eve were driven out of Eden in their case, to guard against it. Thus the purpose of chapters 40 and 41 is to address just this issue. In these, God demonstrates that it is ludicrous to challenge Him, on account of his majesty and strength. God illustrates the point with descriptions of Leviathan and Behemoth. Much comment has been expended discussing whether they are true or real animals or not. But that is beside the point for even if neither existed in Palestine at the time, both the blue whale or a large dinosaur would easily qualify as examples of either. The point is that both were created by God, who in turn controls them. The clear implication of the argument as expressed is that should the gulf between us and one of these creatures be so great, how much more ludicrous it would be to challenge the God who created and controls them. In further notes on chapters 40 and 41 individually I attempt to explain what these two beasts represent and in this present volume seek to enact this in my renderings.   3340   3350

The challenge in this present volume is therefore not to speak about Leviathan and Behemoth but to speak of the challenge to God's majesty that might be offered by someone (like Job) who had suddenly come to appreciate that God exists in a powerful personal sense and yet before such a person had been given the grace to   3360 follow Christ. The wordings in chapters 40 and 41 should therefore continue to be seen as intense challenges to Job.

notes/40

The preceding section assumes that both of the beasts were meant as just that: either actual or mythical beasts but which are both proxies for God's unimaginable power. The presented text for ch 40 in this current volume has plainly gone in a different direction. I now attempt to explain why.   3370

40.16 and 17 are speaking of the fecundity of the beast in the sense of "see how reproductively successful this beast is". In our own culture such talk even in academic circles rarely goes beyond the purile. In Ancient Hebrew culture, reproductive success was seen as a profound blessing whereas an inability either to have children or to have large flocks and herds, was seen as a curse. In order to understand this ch 40 we must try to disassociate our own deeply ingrained cultural thought that sex is dark, dangerous and dirty and appreciate that when restored to its rightful place and to its domain   3380 in life, it becomes a sacred space of God's blessing. Precisely because it is a sacred space it's fences are not to be breached else on pain of severe sanction: it can only be approached by the appropriate individuals of the respective species and through the appropriate gate.

Next and as a general rule, we must remember that words have resonance and where heard in different contexts to that in which they are otherwise heard, retain or even amplify that resonance. If I start saying "we shall not grow old ..." to a British audience (and there will be similar phrases with similar resonances in other   3390 languages to nations worldwide), I would expect them to associate those words with the annual Remembrance ceremonies. That is what makes them respected and special.

I submit that the word Behemoth to a Hebrew speaking audience would bring to mind another: *byhemah* (see Gen 1.24; see NET bible notes for Job 40 in this section and also for Genesis 1) which in the context of Genesis 1 speaks of the blessing of voluminous herds of cattle and other domesticated animals.

Finally we must be comfortable with a text having multiple layers of meaning: it is not that one is right and another wrong or again that   3400 one meaning is necessarily more important than another or even that there is a precession of meaning: no, it is like a modern-day hologram, it really is one thing to one way of seeing it and another to another.

Thus and taken together we have, I would submit, God revealing to Job His divine powers as demonstrated in Genesis 1 but in a new way. Genesis 1 does not reveal "God, the Lord" but simply God, *Elohim*. Job is now encountering the personal God (see ch. 42.5) and with a closer approach to a fearsome holy God, comes far, far greater responsibility to honour God as God. It is the difference   3410
between seeing a smoking volcano from an aircraft 10 miles away and to being on the lip of the caldera feeling the heat and light of the surging, molten, heaving magma, strip away your protective suit.

notes/41

In ch.40 God spoke to Job of a mystery than humanity at least can see, the blessing of bounty in the abundance of cattle and animals. The challenge to Job was plainly that none of this could he influence or understand in anyway.

In ch.41 God challenges Job with something that humanity rarely   3420
sees: the apparent immensity of the ferocity of the natural world, especially of the oceans and with that of how humanity is effectively cosseted to a considerable extent away from such natural dangers. In our generation we might also think of for example the Van Allen belts which shield the earth and its inhabitants from damaging radiation. Similarly the earth appears to be located in a region of space where energetic events and bodies are not quite as populous as they are elsewhere - again it would seem that we are in a form of oasis of calm in an otherwise raucously dangerous Universe. Again, even our explorations of space at this early stage of our interstellar   3430
development demonstrate how dangerous the environment of space is and the extraordinary lengths in equipment, in training, in cost, we have as humans to go to, in order to protect ourselves.

We can also appreciate this oasis of calm from our own earthly vantage point: shark attacks are fortunately rare and arguably humans are to a degree responsible simply by being places it might be wise not to be and yet footage of these animals reveals just what they can do and the raw energy of their ferocity. Yet this phenomenon is also revealed I would suggest in a more paradoxical way: immense whales almost at times seem to caress   3440
or play with tourists going out to view them, their very gentleness

when confronted by flimsy boats merely serving to underline what they are capable of in for example their battles in the depths with the octopus which some whales take for food.

Thus Leviathan is proxy for all that humanity cannot control of the natural environment and of the mysterious placing, the cosmic locating of this environment in which we live, by God for our thriving.

notes/42

Job declares that up until this point he had only known of God 'by the hearing of the ear' (42.5) but now as a result of God's words to him, he states that, 'my eye sees you'. This final declaration demonstrates the objective of the entire book as Job comes to repent. God declares that Job has spoken correctly unlike his friends. Job is justified by God as the friends offer sacrifice and he Job prays for them (Job 42.7-10). These statements also bring the journey of Job towards his Creator to a resolution.

An Annotated Bibliography

Alter, Robert, 2010. *The Wisdom Books: A Translation with Commentary.* New York: W W Norton.

The New American Standard Bible (revision of 1995)

First edition NET bible and notes.

Jerome Commentary

Printed in Poland
by Amazon Fulfillment
Poland Sp. z o.o., Wrocław

86035082R00063